To Better Health

42 DAYS

TO

A NEW LIFE

**The Importance of a Balanced Fat Intake
That Will Change Your Health
(From Alpha to Omega)**

M. Frank Lyons II, M.D.

xulon
PRESS

Dedication

The need to help my patients better understand their nutritional health as it relates to their medical conditions has prompted and encouraged me to complete this book so that I may better serve their medical needs. I dedicate this book to all my patients, past, present and future, with my sincere thanks.

Acknowledgements

I would like to thank my many family members, friends and colleagues who have put up with my constant iterations about this topic for the past decade as I have been gathering information in preparation for the writing of this book.

A special thanks to my sister Debbie Shucka for constantly encouraging me and assisting in the preparation of the manuscript.

Others who were a great help to me in the editing process include: Maggie Steenrod, Mary Varon, Dr. William Hirota, and Dr. Michael Kimmey. I very much appreciate all their criticisms and suggestions to improve this message.

I am greatly indebted to my wonderful wife, Clare who saw me through the ups and downs of completing this project. Without her patience, encouragement and vision, it would still be unfinished.

Finally, I want to thank God for bringing me to the point of understanding this complex, yet vital topic concerning the care of my patients.

"Did you ever observe to whom accidents happen? Chance favors the prepared mind."

Louis Pasteur

Table of Contents

"Wisdom is proved right by all its results."
Luke 7:35

Introduction

A registered nurse came to see me for recurring upper abdominal pain and heartburn. She was referred to me by her primary care physician. I am a gastroenterologist, a doctor who specializes in the evaluation and management of gastrointestinal disorders. My evaluation of the patient revealed that she was suffering from gallbladder dysfunction, a hiatal hernia, and gastroesophageal reflux disease. I attempted to treat her conditions with medications and life-style changes. She began consuming over $12 of medications daily, and she was eating a low-fat, high-fiber, low-caffeine diet without any appreciable success in controlling her symptoms.

After several months of trying medications and dietary modifications without success, the two of us came to the conclusion that her only option was to undergo surgery to remove her gallbladder and have her hiatal hernia repaired. She was referred to a surgeon, and an operation date was set. While awaiting surgery, the woman was so miserable with her ongoing symptoms that she consulted the internet for some temporary relief. Her research led her to begin ingesting flax seed oil.

> **She emphatically stated to me, "42 days on flax seed oil gave me my life back! I have a new life without symptoms." What she received after 42 days was a new life without pain and there was no need for further medication or surgery.**

By the time her surgery date arrived, her symptoms had totally abated; she was off all medications, and she cancelled the surgery. **Six weeks later (42 days)** she returned to my office for her follow-up office visit and related this story to me. She told me that she didn't even know what flax seed oil was or what was in it but she knew that she was cured. She strongly encouraged me to find out why.

What does **"42 days"** have to do with this book? The first patient that prompted me to begin my exploration of flax seed oil, and omega-3 fatty acids, saw me **42 days** after she began taking flax seed oil for her intestinal problems. Of note, all her symptoms resolved over that **42 day** period, and she was given a new lease on life. Some of the problems caused by a deficiency of the essential fatty acid known as omega-3 fat can respond to treatment quicker than **42 days**, such as joint pain, or longer than **42 days**, such as heart disease and cancer. Regardless of the number of days, we all need to get our essential fat intake back into balance in order to enjoy the health of our ancestors.

This book is written to educate you about the biggest epidemic to affect America in its entire history. This epidemic is the fat imbalance in our diet. It has plagued most Americans for the past 75 years.

The industrial revolution brought many wonderful innovations that have changed our lives forever: internal combustion engines, automobiles, refrigeration, electric motors, electric power, and tele-communication, and so on. The list is endless. The same technology also brought about the commercialization of food production. The process, known as partial hydrogenation of fat was developed. At that time in American history, refrigeration was substandard, and preservation of fresh food was paramount to survival. The partial hydrogenation process prevented food from spoiling, especially fats.

What appeared to be a major improvement in food preservation now proves to be the beginning of the erosion of fat balance of the American diet. That fat imbalance has led to the greatest health problem that has ever been recorded in the United States. Countless Americans have suffered and died due to this misfortune of history. Many more are presently suffering its consequences. By the time you have completed reading this book, you will have a new appreciation of the importance of restoring the balance of your fatty acid intake. Then you can get started on your own **"42 day"** journey toward better health.

"Healthy people don't need a doctor, those who are sick do." Matthew 9:12

Chapter 1

Essential Fatty Acid Deficiency

Fifty years ago, I grew up in the northern panhandle of the state of Idaho. It was an area of America that was filled with family dairy farms, logging communities and a rural lifestyle. We all cultivated large gardens, orchards, and berry patches. We consumed meat and dairy products that were locally produced. The four distinct seasons caused us to dearly enjoy the short, summer months. We never lacked for food on the table, we drank primarily milk and spring water, and we ate farm and garden produce daily. Yet we lived very healthy lives. Only one boy in my high school class suffered from juvenile diabetes. To the best of my knowledge, the rest of us did not have any diseases, mental illness, or other chronic conditions. Our parents did not suffer from heart disease or cancer, and the senior citizens lived to old age without significant maladies. Times have changed. Today, children suffer from mental disorders and diabetes, cancer affecting all ages is rampant, and people take pills by the dozen daily in an attempt to reduce complications of all sorts of diseases.

Is there a medical explanation for the explosion of American ailments? Juvenile depression, peripheral neuropathy, attention deficit disorder, fibromyalgia, fatty liver, rampant rates of cancer of the colon, breast and prostate, skin problems, atherosclerotic heart disease, and adolescent dysmenorrhea are among the medical conditions rising in all races and genders across America.

The answer may lie in a disease first described in the 1920's known now as **essential fatty acid deficiency**. Insights into this disease were unearthed when it was demonstrated that a small amount of dietary fat was necessary for laboratory rats to reproduce, grow normally, and live healthy lives. In 1929, Burr and Burr demonstrated that linoleic acid (an omega-6 polyunsaturated fatty acid) was the essential nutrient for the rat to retain these functions in health. In the rat, essential fatty acid deficiency went on to be described as a disease manifest by cessation of growth, dermatitis, excessive skin loss of water, loss of blood in the urine, fatty liver, and loss of reproductive capacity.

Two essential fatty acids are needed for life:
- **Omega-3 Fat**
- **Omega-6 Fat**

The essential fatty acids, linoleic acid (omega-6) and alpha-linolenic acid (omega-3) are long-chain polyunsaturated fatty acids that are now known to be necessary for normal fetal development, childhood and adolescent growth and functioning. Both of these fats are the parent compounds for their respective omega classes of fats needed to maintain body function. This was not understood in the 1920's. It is also now known that these fats are needed in the diet because animals or humans cannot make either fatty acid. It has taken 75 years for the scientific community to unravel the mysteries surrounding essential fatty acids. Much is still being learned about the terrible damage suffered by the human body with continued deficiency or unbalanced ingestion of these fats.

In the early nineteenth century, British doctors realized that children were much healthier when their diets were supplemented with fish oil (cod liver oil). It is now known that cod liver oil is rich in Vitamin D. Ingestion of this vitamin prevents rickets (a bone disease marked by bone distortion and bending). This dietary supplement was brought to America in the early twentieth century and the United States government mandated its consumption by children daily until the early 1960's. I can recall ingesting cod liver oil until that time. The Food and Drug Administration subsequently mandated the supplementation of Vitamin A and Vitamin D in milk in order to prevent rickets (vitamin D) and blindness (vitamin A). Subsequently, cod liver oil was no longer recommended as a dietary supplement for a source of vitamin D. Unfortunately, this was also a major source of essential fatty acids in the modern Western diet as America does not consume many of the foods rich in omega-3 and omega-6 fatty acids. Since that time, clinical manifestations now attributed to essential fatty acid deficiency have become increasingly more prevalent in America.

What are these clinical manifestations? Insights into this question have only begun to be unraveled in the past 25 years. With the development of intravenous feeding formulas, it was soon realized that tube feeding devoid of fat rapidly led to liver abnormalities, gallbladder stone formation, skin problems, neurologic symptoms, and even death with sustained intravenous feeding that had no essential fat supplementation. Subsequent studies utilizing various intravenous fat formulas demonstrated that these abnormalities could be prevented.

Additionally, self-imposed diets excluding any fats have led to multiple skin problems, lethargy and fatigue, development of a fatty liver, worsening of diabetes and blood pressure control, and depression. These symptoms develop rapidly in individuals when they take essential fats out of their diet. Liver and gallbladder abnormalities can develop in days to weeks. Some of the other problems may take weeks to months to develop. It also appears that these manifestations are usually reversible in the otherwise healthy adult when the diet is then supplemented with essential fatty acids. In the fetus, infant or developing child, it is less clear at this time whether the abnormalities caused by essential fatty acid deficiency can be corrected later in life with dietary supplementation. For example, it is now established that breast feeding leads to a higher intelligence level as measured by various intelligence testing methods. Breast milk is rich in essential fatty acids. It is not known whether this fatty acid deficit can be overcome in children not receiving these nutrients from breast milk through subsequent dietary supplementation.

Numerous nutrients are required for growth and maintenance of the human body. In long-term health, the essential fatty acids are very important. Prolonged deficiency of essential fatty acids will ultimately lead to death. In the short term, poor growth, learning disability, poor vision, skin problems, attention deficit disorder, degenerative joint diseases, prostate problems, gallbladder dysfunction, cardiovascular disease, mental disorders, and the potential for increased risk of cancer formation are some of the documented problems.

As a gastroenterologist, I can relate numerous testimonies from patients concerning the importance and benefits of omega-3 fat supplementation. The first time I was made aware of the problems related to essential fatty acid deficiency and clinical illness was when the nurse of whom I spoke earlier educated me about her success with flax seed oil. After 10 years of studying flax seed oil, essential fatty acids, Trans fats and their importance in health and disease, the result is this book. This endeavor is an attempt to help educate people about the importance of essential fatty acids in establishing and maintaining healthier bodies. Subsequent chapters will help the reader to understand the role of fat in health and disease and the differences between "good" and "bad" fats.

Pearls

- **Fat is essential for life**
- **Omega-3 and Omega-6 fatty acids are required for life**
- **Deficiency or imbalance of essential fatty acids causes disease**

"Pay attention to what you are listening to, knowledge will be measured out to you by the measure of attention you give. This is the way knowledge increases." Mark 4:24

Chapter 2

"Essential" Means "Essential"

What does it mean when you hear the word **essential**? In the context of living a healthy life, **essential** means something that is required to sustain normal function of the human body. Sleep is an example of something that is needed to maintain health. Without sleep the mind and body pay a heavy price. The mind becomes confused, and the body becomes severely fatigued. If this deprivation continues, one can become psychotic, and the body can completely shut down. After several days of sleep deprivation, a person will die.

When one thinks about the word **essential** as it relates to nutrition, it becomes clear that there are fundamental truths about what is required to maintain normal body function. The first of these is water. The majority of the human body is composed of this **essential** molecule. Without water a person can sustain life for only a few days before succumbing to dehydration and death.

Food is also required for the body to sustain itself. The basic components of food include: vitamins, minerals, carbohydrates, proteins, and fats. Not all constituents of food are necessary to maintain health. An example of this is carbohydrates, which are sugar compounds. Those most familiar to the reader are the starches (potatoes, rice), sugars (table sugar, honey), celluloses (fruits, vegetables), and gums (certain plants). While foods containing carbohydrates may contain essential nutrients such as vitamins and minerals that benefit the body, there are no **essential** carbohydrates necessary to maintain health. The body has the ability to make all the carbohydrates (primarily glucose) to carry out normal function. Unfortunately, the majority of the western diet is composed of carbohydrates. This has led to weight problems, elevated blood cholesterol problems, and numerous medical ailments (heart disease, strokes, cancer, and diabetes, to name a few).

As omnivores, consumers of plants and animals, we enjoy many carbohydrates, and many of the unprocessed plants containing carbohydrates also contain numerous essential elements. Because of this, these plants should be included in the balanced diet.

The majority of the carbohydrates that we consume are found in processed foods, and many of these sugars are nutritionally detrimental. The carbohydrates of fresh fruits and vegetables are quite beneficial to our health.

Vitamins are familiar to most people. It has been recognized for centuries that there were substances in foods that were necessary for good health. In the early part of the twentieth century, research led to the isolation and identification of molecules (first called "vital amines") that are now known as vitamins. While not all vitamins are "amines," they are all vital for normal health (see Table 1).

Diseases may appear in only weeks to months of a diet deficient in vitamins. The best known disease due to vitamin deficiency is scurvy caused by a deficiency of vitamin C. Likewise, it may take months to years for the wrath of vitamin deficiency to become apparent. Rickets following vitamin D deficiency; night blindness from vitamin A deficiency; and dementia, neuropathy and anemia due to vitamin B12 deficiency are a few of these examples. Vitamins are easily acquired either through a balanced diet or through vitamin supplementation. Because of this, vitamin deficiency-related disease is quite rare today in America.

Table 1. Essential Vitamins of the Human Body.

Vitamin	Richest Sources	RDA*	Effect of Deficiency
A (Retinol)	dairy products, halibut, cod, carrots, pumpkin, cantaloupe, tomatoes, spinach, peaches, eggs, peppers, yams, broccoli, squash, broccoli, grapefruit, sweet potato	5000 IU**	night blindness, skin/eye/mouth dryness
B1 (Thiamine)	pork, beef, sunflower seeds, peas, orange juice, bran flakes	1-1.5 mg***	muscle wasting, heart failure, nerve damage, brain degeneration
B2 (Riboflavin)	liver, pork, milk products, beef, green leafy vegetables, eggs	1.1-1.8 mg	light sensitivity, cracks in the corner of the mouth
B3 (Niacin)	liver, tuna, turkey, chicken, salmon, red meat, peanuts, milk products, asparagus, legumes	12-20 mg	pellegra, delirium, sore tongue
B5 (Pantothenic Acid)	widespread in foods	5-10 mg	vomiting, fatigue, insomnia, indigestion, hypoglycemia

B6 (Pyridoxine)	meats, fish, poultry, liver, legumes, fruits, potatoes	1-2 mg	rash, dermatitis, anemia, convulsions
B7 (Biotin)	widespread in foods	100-200 mcg#	abnormal heart rhythm, anorexia, weakness, depression
B9 (Folic Acid)	asparagus, avocado, beets, green leafy vegetables, seeds legumes, liver	400 mcg	frequent infections, cancer
B12 (Cobalamin)	animal meats, milk, cheese, eggs	3 mcg	dementia, anemia, neuropathy
C (Ascorbic Acid)	citrus fruit, cabbage, tomatoes, dark green vegetables, potatoes	75-90 mg	scurvy
D (Ergocalciferol)	sunlight, fortified milk, liver, sardines, salmon, shrimp	400 IU	rickets, osteomalacia
E (Alpha-tocopherol)	polyunsaturated plant fat oil, green leafy vegetables, wheat germ, nuts, seeds	33 IU	nerve degeneration, weakness, leg cramps, difficulty walking
K (Phylloquinone)	bacterial synthesis in GI tract, soy beans, vegetable oils, green leafy vegetables	50-100 mcg	bleeding, decreased clotting

*RDA: recommended daily allowance; **IU: international units; ***mg: milligrams; #mcg: micrograms.

Minerals are not as well understood by the reader. Minerals are inorganic elements found in nature that come from the soil. These nutrients are required in many aspects of normal health. Iron is probably the best-known mineral. Without iron in the diet, one becomes severely anemic. Red blood cells require iron to carry oxygen to the body. Copper, zinc, sodium, calcium, magnesium, phosphorus, and potassium are other well-known examples of minerals. Sustained mineral deficiency in any one of these minerals is not compatible with life.

Protein is also **essential** in building and maintaining a healthy body. Protein is made up of amino acids. There are 20 **essential** amino acids required by the body. These amino acids are required to make and maintain muscles, body enzymes, immunoglobulins, albumin, and many other body components. Without protein containing these 20 amino acids, the body will eventually fail. High quality protein can be found in meats (beef, fish, and poultry), eggs, milk products, and some vegetables (soy, beans, and lentils).

Fats are the last group of molecules that are **essential** to maintain health in the human body. While there are many kinds of fats found in nature and the human body, there are only two fats found in nature that the body cannot make on its own. Both of these fats are polyunsaturated fatty acids (see later text for further explanation). The two types of polyunsaturated fatty acids found in the body that must be ingested are omega-6 fatty acids (safflower oil, corn oil) and omega-3 fatty acids (fish oil, flax oil). Our Westernized diet is deficient in omega-3 fatty acids. Deficiency in these oils leads to a number of maladies in the body. While omega-6 fatty acid deficiency has been understood fairly well since the 1920's, omega-3 fatty acid deficiency is only now beginning to be recognized as a major health problem in America.

I recently saw a 17-year-old young woman in my office accompanied by her mother for an appointment. She was suffering from gallbladder and irritable bowel problems. She is a typical teenager. She eats fast foods regularly. She has a diet that contains almost no omega-3 fats.

After I completed her diagnostic workup I attempted to educate her about the importance of her paying attention to her diet. To my chagrin, the information was going in one ear and out the other.

I then took another direction in my attempt to reach this young woman. Understanding the emphasis placed on personal appearance by most young people, I took advantage of that fact. I asked her if she liked her breasts. She asked what I meant. I asked her if she wanted to keep her breasts intact. She said, "Definitely." I had her attention. I informed her that her diet, deficient in omega-3 fatty acid, could decide whether she would become one of the millions of women in America who eventually develop breast cancer. Cancer that could lead to the removal of a part or all of a breast.

Both she and her mom quickly grasped the gravity of the knowledge I was trying to impart. You see, they have family members who have suffered from the ravages of breast cancer. The girl promised me that she would take a more active role in her diet. She kept her word. She went on to write a research paper on the importance of omega-3 fats for a school project. She changed her diet, and this has drastically reduced her intestinal problems.

The purpose of this book is to help bring a simple understanding to a very complex and confusing subject: Omega-3 fatty acid deficiency and fatty acid imbalance in the American diet.

When a person is diagnosed with a medical condition in modern America, the solution is to treat that condition with a pill, a medical procedure, or a surgery. While there are some medical conditions not directly related to our diet (infectious diseases, inherited disorders, etc.), many of the health problems found in America today are directly related to our diet. The solution in these individuals should have been to prevent the medical condition in the first place. At the forefront of American health care should be educating the person about the role of ingesting a diet containing **all** of the **essential** elements (see Table 2) required to maintain health.

Table 2. Nutritional Elements "Essential" for a Healthy Body

Water (Lots)
Vitamins (13 of them)
Minerals (several)
Protein (20 amino acids)
Fat (omega-3, omega-6)

Omega-3 fatty acid deficiency plays a poorly recognized, but major role in the health problems facing America today. After reading the rest of this book, you will be able to understand how to prevent this fatty acid deficiency. More importantly though, it will be clear to you why you would **want** to prevent fatty acid deficiency. Just as my teenage patient took charge of her diet to reduce her symptoms, so too we all can eat better if we want to live healthier lives.

Pearls

- **"Essential" means "Essential"**
- **The body needs water, vitamins, minerals, protein and fat**
- **The two essential fats are omega-3 and omega-6 fat**

"In the house of the wise are stores of choice food
and oil, but a foolish man devours all he has."
Proverbs 21:20

Chapter 3

Nuggets on Nutrition

What happens when you eat a meal? Where does the food go? How is the food digested? The questions could be endless. The purpose of this chapter is to help the reader understand how digestion occurs.

Digestion begins with chewing of food. The initial grinding of the food in the mouth and the mixing of salivary digestive juices are not essential to digestion. However, people who suffer from the inability to produce saliva have a difficult time swallowing their food. Additionally, if one has no teeth or suffers from severe periodontal disease, this individual is markedly limited in his/her choices of food that can be easily ingested due to an inability to chew the food. This inadequacy can potentially lead to choking, obstructing the airways, or blocking the passageway of the esophagus.

Mr. S. was a 74-year-old man who came into my office complaining of difficulty swallowing his food. He stated that the problem had been present for several years. He asked, "Doctor, is there anything that you could do to help me?" A thorough examination revealed a small stricture or narrowing of his esophagus, the tube going from the mouth to the stomach. Upon fixing this problem, Mr. S. could swallow his food and he was ecstatic. He no longer worried about eating solid foods and because he loved to go fishing in the Puget Sound, he could now eat all the salmon he wanted. He was catching his Omega-3's and eating them too!

Once food is swallowed, it passes down the esophagus into the stomach. The stomach serves many functions. It acts as a storage room for recently ingested food. The normal stomach in an adult holds approximately 1.5 to 2 liters. The stomach continues the grinding process initiated in the mouth. During the grinding process, a small amount of the food is released into the small intestine in intermittent, controlled intervals. While there is only a small amount of digestion that occurs in the stomach, one can live without a stomach and still maintain normal nutrition. The one major exception to this statement is that the stomach is required for vitamin B-12 release from food and it's binding to a protein (intrinsic factor) produced by the stomach. This vitamin B-12-protein complex is protected from further digestion in the remainder of the intestine and will eventually be absorbed in the last part of the small intestine (ileum). The stomach produces hydrochloric acid. This acid plays a small role in the digestive process by providing the optimum pH for initial enzyme activity to occur in the stomach. More importantly, however, this acid inhibits growth of many ingested microorganisms.

Food is slowly released from the stomach into the small intestine. The overall length of the small intestine is approximately 14 feet. The small intestine has three parts: the duodenum, the jejunum, and the ileum. The absorptive surface area of the small intestine, if spread out flat, would cover the entire surface of a single's tennis court. The duodenum receives small quantities of food from the stomach in timed intervals. Vital functions occur in this segment of small bowel. Folic acid and iron (see Chapter 2) are absorbed here. Additionally, mixing of food with bile and pancreatic juices occurs in the duodenum. These juices are absolutely necessary for the digestive process, but very little absorption of the digested nutrients is absorbed here.

Bile is produced in the liver and is stored in the gallbladder during times of fasting. Bile serves as a detergent for fat. It allows fat to go into a water solution much like soap cuts grease in the kitchen sink. This process is known as emulsification. Fat cannot be absorbed unless it is emulsified into a water solution.

Pancreatic juices contain several key ingredients necessary for digestion. The first of these is bicarbonate. This neutralizes acidic juice coming out of the stomach. It also serves as a pH buffer that allows digestive juices present in the lining of the intestine and those released by the pancreas to be activated. The pancreas also produces digestive enzymes for each of the major food components (carbohydrates, fats, proteins). These enzymes are named amylase, lipase, and proteases. Amylase begins the breakdown of starches, lipase the breakdown of fats, and proteases the breakdown of proteins.

As food is mixed with bile and pancreatic juices in the duodenum, the digestive process is underway. Starches, fats, and proteins are broken down to smaller molecules that can then be either absorbed across the jejunal (second part of the small intestine) wall into the bloodstream or are further digested by enzymes found in the intestinal lining. Once the food particles are broken down to a size that can be carried into the bloodstream, nearly all of these nutrients are transported into the intestinal bloodstream and taken to the liver. Only bile salts (a component of bile) and vitamin B-12 are absorbed in the last part of the small intestine called the ileum. The colon plays no significant role in digestion other than to absorb water, collect indigestible food products/wastes, and store it until it is excreted as feces.

Digested food is absorbed across the intestinal lining, and it is carried to the liver by the abdominal blood vessels. These digested sugar, fat, and protein sub-particles undergo numerous metabolic transformations as the body demands. These demands may include tissue healing, tissue/body growth, infection control, and energy storage for a "rainy day," thinking, exercising, and even sleeping. Synthesis of albumin and other proteins, clotting factors, storage sugar (glycogen), and waste products (such as urea from nitrogen waste) are just a few of these processes. The liver also metabolizes medications, detoxifies environmental chemicals, and alcohol, and is involved with packaging vitamins A and vitamin D.

When excess calories are ingested, the liver converts excess sugar into glycogen and stores this in the liver and muscles. Once these organs' glycogen storage capacity has been reached, all extra calories of fat, sugar, or proteins are converted to fat. This fat can be stored in the abdomen, subcutaneous area of the skin, and in the liver itself. During prolonged fasting, the first calories mobilized to meet body requirements for energy are glycogen stores from the liver. Once glycogen is depleted, fat stores are mobilized, and the patient begins to lose weight. Muscle wasting will also occur if fasting is continued, and/or if demands for body proteins occur.

Pearls

- **Digestion is a complex process**
- **A healthy digestive system optimizes proper nutrition**

"When I tried to understand all this, it was oppressive to me." Psalm 73:16

Chapter 4

Understanding the Inflammation – Fat Connection

We had just arrived on the big island of Hawaii and our teenage children and their friends were itching to get to the beach and start working on their tans. In spite of urgent requests by those with common sense (the parents) the young men did not feel that they needed to apply protective lotions prior to a day of harsh, tropical solar baking. That evening the male adolescents began to look like freshly cooked lobsters. The skin of their upper torsos was ruby red, hot, and intensely tender to the touch. For the next three days they had to stay out of sight of the sunny skies radiating over the beaches of Kona. Why did their bodies react in this way? This was a classic protective mechanism programmed into their DNA known as acute (rapid response) inflammatory reaction. The ultraviolet rays of the sun struck their skin and initiated a damaging process that, without an acute inflammatory reaction, would lead to their ultimate death.

You see, the inflammatory reaction acts outwardly to warn us of the damage that has been brought against our bodies. This is the pain, fever, redness, and swelling that occurs with acute inflammation. Inwardly, it serves to rid the human body of the damage brought on by the injurious agent. This process attempts to stop the injury, clean up the damaged areas of the body, and repair the body back to a functional state. Often, the repair process can lead to scar formation (known as fibrosis) in the injured body part rather than regeneration of the originally damaged tissue.

Injurious agents to the human body include:

- **Chemical injury** (*alcohol, illegal street drugs, pharmaceuticals*)
- **Foreign bodies** (*dirty needles, splinters, bullets*)
- **Immunologic reactions** (*bee stings, food allergies*)
- **Irradiation** (*radio-active substance exposure, ultraviolet rays, x-rays*)
- **Ischemic injury** (*heart attack, stroke, shock, rapid blood loss*)
- **Microbes** (*viruses, bacteria, fungi, protozoa, rickettsia*)
- **Thermal injury** (*burns, frostbite, sunburn*)
- **Toxins** (*biologic, chemical*)
- **Trauma** (*penetrating, blunt, crush*)

The inflammatory process was first described by the Egyptians around 3000 B.C. The understanding of the four cardinal features of inflammation (heat, pain, redness, and swelling) is attributed to the first century Roman writer Celsus.

It was not until the 18th century, however, that inflammation was recognized as a response to an injurious agent rather than a disease.

A rudimentary understanding about the processes involved in inflammation began to be described during the 19th century with the description of phagocytosis and serum factors needed to fight off injurious agents. Phagocytosis is the process where certain types of white blood cells (macrophages) surround, engulf and destroy an injurious agent (such as a bacterium). Serum factors were later determined to be antibodies. Antibodies are proteins produced by white blood cells in response to exposure to a potentially harmful substance that enters our body. These proteins can attach to the harmful agent (virus, bacteria, etc.) and neutralize the agent or lead to its death.

Since the discovery of the AIDS (HIV) virus in the mid 1980's, an explosion of knowledge surrounding the understanding of the inflammatory and immune processes has expanded geometrically. The tools (computers, DNA sequencing, chromatography, ultracentrifuges, electron microscopy, etc.) developed to understand the biochemistry, molecular biology and genetics of the human body during this time period has led to more understanding of inflammation and immunity than all previously known knowledge in recorded history.

The inflammatory process is divided into acute and chronic inflammation. Acute inflammation develops rapidly after exposure to the injurious agent (see above list). This reaction can occur in seconds to minutes. The inflammatory process lasts a short time and typically is resolved in a few days. If you think about our sunburned young men mentioned at the outset of this chapter, their lobster-like skin was well on its way to bronzing (or peeling in this case) within a few days of the ultraviolet injury. Chronic inflammation, on the other hand, is a process that lasts much longer (weeks to years). It can lead to significant damage to the human body such as is seen with tuberculosis, rheumatoid arthritis, Crohn's disease, atherosclerotic heart disease, and cancers.

Inflammation is halted only when several events occur. These events are:

- **Elimination of the injurious agent**
- **Healing of the injured area of the body**
- **Prevention of continued inflammation by anti-inflammatory factors**

If any of these factors is not accomplished, chronic inflammation persists and injury persists. This continued injury can lead to irreversible damage to the body (lung fibrosis, cirrhosis of the liver, cancer, heart attacks, etc.) and death of the organ or entire human body.

As mentioned above, the body has mechanisms to eliminate the injurious agent (phagocytosis, antibodies). After the injurious agent has been neutralized, destroyed or removed from the body, tissue repair proceeds. This healing process requires three responses in the injured area: regeneration or rebuilding of the cells involved in the injury (skin, liver, etc.); healing (removal of debris from cell death, pus formation, etc.), and scar formation. Where the regenerating cells are unable to restore the normal tissue architecture, scar tissue fills in the damaged area like a patch on a tire inner tube. If the body can restore all of the damaged area with normal structures (skin with only new skin cells, etc.), then there is complete tissue restitution without scarring. A mild to moderate sunburn can lead to complete restitution; however, continued, recurrent injury can cause DNA damage that may progress to cancer formation.

Why do you need to understand this long lead-in to a connection between fat and inflammation? Fat plays an absolutely vital role in the regulation of inflammation, both acute and chronic. The inflammatory process requires an initiation process and an inhibition process in order for the injured area to be both protected from the injurious agent and healed once the inflammatory process is initiated. Both are necessary. If no initiation of the inflammatory reaction occurs, the injurious agent could overwhelm the exposed area to the point where survival is threatened. Once inflammation is underway, the body needs to shut down this process, or chronic inflammation, significant body damage and eventually death may ensue.

The initiation and discontinuation of inflammation is regulated by inflammatory factors produced by the body. They include substances known as cytokines, prostaglandins, leukotrienes, and tumor necrosis factor. The body has pro-inflammatory and anti-inflammatory factors that work to balance the initiation and resolution of the inflammatory process. Omega-6 fatty acids are required for the synthesis of the pro-inflammatory factors while the omega-3 fatty acids are needed for the production of the anti-inflammatory substances (see Figure 1). One without the other can lead to chaos in the regulation of the inflammatory process.

Figure 1. The connection between essential fatty acids and inflammation.

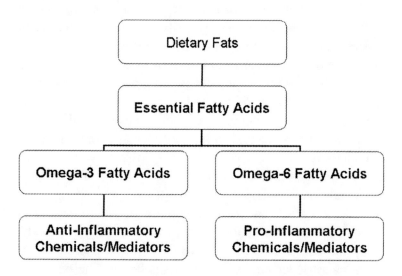

Omega-6 fatty acid ingestion without a balance of omega-3 fatty acid leads to chronic inflammation (see Figure 2). Animals supplemented with too much omega-6 fats causes an increased production of pro-inflammatory mediators that will produce altered immune reactions, chronic inflammatory states that lead to tissue destruction, deformity, and cancer formation and death. Much epidemiologic (population-based) data and human studies reveal similar findings relating to omega-6 fat ingestion that is excessively out of balance with omega-3 fat ingestion.

Excess omega-3 fat feeding in animal models has led to decreased survival or prolonged infection following a few bacterial infections. I think it is important to note, though, that only excess omega-6 fat has been shown to be a problem in humans, while no data suggests a problem with excess omega-3 fats.

Several population studies reveal just the opposite. Diets that are rich in omega-3 fatty acids dramatically reduce the incidence of heart disease, chronic inflammatory diseases, chronic immune disorders and cancer, while omega-3 fat deficient diets cause just the opposite (see Figure 2).

The frequency of these disorders has exploded in America in the past 100 years. This is because our diet is lopsided with excess omega-6 fat and is desperately deficient in omega-3 fat.

Figure 2. The Role of essential fatty acids in the inflammatory process.

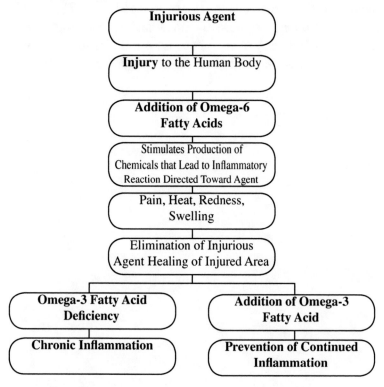

Prior to the 20th century, the American diet consisted of one- to two-parts of omega-3 fat to one part omega-6 fat. By the end of the century the ratio had changed to one-part omega-3 fat to 20 parts omega-6 fats. Additionally, most of the omega-3 fat had been removed from our diet. Worse than that, much of the omega-6 fat was Trans fat (see next chapter). This change in the Westernized diet has led to a rapid increase in the chronic inflammatory diseases and cancer in America (see Table 1).

Table 1. Diseases caused by chronic inflammation.

Organ	Diseases
Blood Vessels	Stroke, heart attack, intestinal ischemia
Bones	Rheumatoid arthritis, osteoarthritis, osteoporosis
Brain	ADD/ADHD, autism, depression, dementia
Breast	Fibrocystic breasts, breast cancer
Colon/Intestine	Colitis, Crohn's disease, colon cancer
Eyes	Decreased vision, macular degeneration
Immune System	Autoimmune disease, lymphoma
Liver	Hepatitis (some types), cirrhosis, liver cancer
Prostate	Chronic prostatitis, prostate cancer
Skin	Psoriasis, acne, seborrhea, eczema, skin cancer

The dietary source of fatty acids is critical in determining the quantity and the type (omega-3, omega-6, saturated fat, etc.) of fat ingested. Most vegetable oils (other than flax seed oil and canola oil) are rich in omega-6 fat. Omega-3 fat rich foods are found primarily in cold-water ocean fish (salmon, herring, etc.), shellfish, green leafy vegetables, flax seed, and rapeseed (canola oil). The levels of the omega fats in farm animals and dairy products vary depending on the diet of the animals. For example, if chickens are fed a diet rich in corn meal (omega-6 fat), their meat and eggs will be rich in omega-6 fatty acid. Conversely, if chickens are fed a diet rich in flax meal (omega-3 fat) they will produce chicken meat and eggs that contain an abundance of omega-3 fat.

What is the significance of this? Switching your diet from one omega-6 egg to one omega-3 egg per day can decrease the omega-6 to omega-3 ratio in your body from 12:1 down to 6:1. If animals are fattened on natural grasses, their meat, eggs, and milk are rich in omega-3 fats. As farm animals were taken out the pastures and placed in feedlots where they were fed corn and grains high in omega-6 fats, we became consumers of farm and dairy products rich in omega-6 fat to the detriment of the omega-3 fats and, ultimately, our health.

As you read chapters 7-14, hopefully, you will grow to understand how this change in our diet has led to these diseases. Additionally, by the end of the book you will have the insight to initiate a dietary change that may not only improve the quality of your health, but it might also help reduce your chances of acquiring a chronic, inflammatory disorder or cancer that could shorten your life.

Pearls

- **Inflammation is essential for health maintenance**
- **Inflammation requires a balance of omega-3 and omega-6 fat in the diet**
- **The American diet has shifted from omega-3 to omega-6 predominance**
- **This shift has led to the many chronic inflammatory disorders seen in America today**

*"Then He will send the rains in their proper
seasons so you can harvest crops of grain, grapes
for wine, and olives for oil." Deuteronomy 11:14*

Chapter 5

Fundamentals of Fats

Fats comprise part of the biologically essential substances
required to maintain human health (see chapters 1, 2).
Fats, also known as lipids, make up about 40% of adult
energy requirements. Lipids occur in nature as cholesterol,
saturated, polyunsaturated, and monounsaturated fats. They
are derived from plants and animals (see Table 1).

**Table 1. Common food sources of the various fats found
in our diet.**

Saturated	Monounsaturated	Omega-3	Omega-6
Beef	*Olive oil*	*Fish*	*Corn oil*
Dairy	*Canola oil (rapeseed)*	*Flaxseed oil*	*Cottonseed oil*
Pork	*Almonds*	*Soybean*	*Soybean*

Saturated	Monounsaturated	Omega-3	Omega-6
Poultry	Nuts (most)	Canola oil	Sunflower
Fish (some)	Sheep	Walnut oil	Sesame oil
Avocado	Rice bran		Peanut oil
Coconut	Fish (some)		Safflower oil
Oysters	Pork		Primrose oil
Nuts (most)	Goose, duck		Borage oil

The composition of plant and animal fats varies depending on the source of nutrition for these organisms (more on this later in the chapter). Polyunsaturated fats are divided into omega-3 and omega-6 fatty acids (see chapter 6). Both of these classes of fatty acids are essential to the diet; that is, we must consume both of them in our diet. If we do not include omega-3, and omega-6 fatty acids regularly, our health suffers in many ways (see chapters 7-15). Omega-6 fats are converted into pro-inflammatory factors, while omega-3 fats are converted to anti-inflammatory substances.

Pro-Inflammatory Factors ← Omega-6 Fat

Omega-3 Fat → Anti-Inflammatory Factors

The human body **requires both of these fats, but in a balanced way**. It is important for the body to defend itself against infections and cell mutations that can lead to cancer.

The inflammatory process allows this defense process to occur.

Inflammation needs to be balanced, however; otherwise the body can severely damage or even destroy itself. Hence, omega-3 fats. They produce the anti-inflammatory factors that offset the inflammatory process. If the human diet consists of too much omega-6 fat compared to omega-3 fat, this pro-inflammatory/anti-inflammatory regulation becomes out of balance and several disease processes develop.

Saturated and monounsaturated fats and cholesterol are not considered essential fats because the human body can manufacture these substances upon demand. While the diet contains these fats, they are not truly detrimental to human health (more on this later in the chapter).

When omega-3 and omega-6 polyunsaturated fats are ingested, they travel to the small intestine where they are absorbed and transported to the liver. Once in the liver, they are converted into a number of compounds that are dispersed throughout the entire body. What is important to understand is that the linoleic acid (omega-6 fatty acid) and alpha linolenic acid (omega-3 fatty) are metabolized by the liver (see Figure 1) through a common enzyme, delta-6 desaturase. They become biologically active precursor molecules involved with cell wall structure. These molecules signal between cells of common interest, insulate between cells, and mediate between pro-inflammatory and anti-inflammatory signaling (see chapter 4).

Figure 1. Essential fatty acids compete for the same enzyme to perform their functions in the human body.

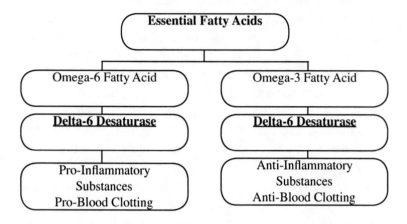

If the liver is overwhelmed with excess ingestion of one omega fat compared with the other, that excess fatty acid gets the majority of the delta-6 desaturase enzyme by sheer competition for the enzyme. In America, our diet strongly favors omega-6 fatty acid ingestion; the manufactured Trans fats in our diet are primarily Trans omega-6 fatty acids as well; and we have nearly completely stripped our diet of any significant measurable omega-3 fatty acids. This combination of events has led to excess ingestion of omega-6 fatty acids. This has resulted in the progression of deadly consequences to our health which you will grow to understand.

Historical Perspective

At the beginning of the twentieth century, the majority of Americans lived on farms. They consumed a diet high in fats, and these fats primarily were of animal origin (over 80% of their fat intake). The fats that these Americans consumed consisted primarily of sheep, beef, fowl, pork, raw whole milk (milk that is not pasteurized and has no cream removed), butter, and eggs. The meat of farm animals grown on pasture land contained high levels of omega-3 fatty acids. Milk and its products (butter, cottage cheese and yogurt) and eggs were also major sources of omega-3 fats. The American diet was rich in fat, and the omega-3 to omega-6 fat ratio in that diet was approximately 1-2:1. Heart disease was a rare event. The first publication concerning thrombosis (the process of clotting of the heart arteries when a person suffers a heart attack) of blood vessels in the heart was not even published until 1912 in the *Journal of the American Medical Association.*

Manufactured Trans Fats

Several changes in fat ingestion occurred in America during the twentieth century that led to a decline in our health.

In 1911, manufactured Trans fat (primarily consisting of partially hydrogenated omega-6 vegetable oil) was introduced into the American food supply by Proctor and Gamble Corporation with the release of Crisco[R] shortening.

Up until that time, cooking oils consisted of saturated, monounsaturated and polyunsaturated vegetable oils (olive oil, corn oil, cottonseed oil, sunflower seed oil, etc.), lard (fat rendered from pork), tallow (fat rendered from beef and sheep), poultry fat, and butter. Vegetable oils were not well suited for baking, and animal fats would become rancid after a relatively short shelf life.

Even though these fats and oils would spoil quickly due to the lack of refrigeration, they had been used for centuries without any significant risks to human health.

Wilhelm Normann, a German chemist, developed the Trans fat process in 1901. He sold the patent to Proctor and Gamble in 1909. The "Normann" Trans fat manufacturing process is a method of converting liquid vegetable polyunsaturated fats into solid fat. This process consists of superheating oil in large vats under pressure to temperatures up to 400° Fahrenheit. Powdered nickel is then mixed with the scalding oil. Hydrogen is then forced into the vat, and the nickel acts as a chemical catalyst to create a Trans fat. The mixture resulting from this process is called "partially hydrogenated fat."

Depending on the initial vegetable oil used in the process, various fat-based products were developed. These included Crisco shortening (partially hydrogenated cottonseed oil), other shortenings, and margarines (partially hydrogenated corn oil, soy bean oil, etc.).

Modern refinements of this hydrogenation process have incorporated alternative metal catalysts such as platinum, cobalt, palladium, and a nickel/aluminum alloy.

The hydrogenation process renders the oil into a solid or semi-solid fatty substance that is flavorless and has **no nutritional value**. These new partially hydrogenated Trans fats have excellent shelf lives, as they are not prone to oxidation and subsequent rancidity. Trans hydrogenated fats are used in the preparation of most dessert products, deep-fried foods (doughnuts, French fries, deep-fried breaded meats, etc.) in the "fast food" industry, potato chips, and crackers.

A steady increase in the consumption of these Trans polyunsaturated fats has led to a significant shift from natural omega-3 fat intake to Trans omega-6 fat ingestion. The reason for this is that the majority of polyunsaturated fats utilized to manufacture Trans fats are vegetable fats rich in omega-6 fats. Trans fats, get incorporated into the membranes of every cell in our bodies. They are difficult to remove by our immune system, and they can remain in the humans for prolonged periods of time. This leads to a number of health problems (see chapters 7-15).

An example of the lack of initial insight into the health risks of chronic Trans fat ingestion came following warnings by Dr. Ancel Keys. A noted Nutrition science professor from the University of Minnesota, he announced to the world in 1958 that chronic ingestion of Trans polyunsaturated fats was the cause of heart disease. The scientific, medical and news media community did not heed his warnings. It was not until 48 years later the *New England Journal of Medicine* published in 2006 a comprehensive review of Trans fat research, concluding that there was, in fact, **a strong and realized connection between heart disease and the consumption of (predominately omega-6) Trans polyunsaturated fat.**

Another major event affecting the consumption of fat occurred in the middle of the 20th century: the **mandatory pasteurization of commercially produced milk** in America.

My father related to me in his later years that there were 56 dairies in my home county in 1958, the year my family moved to a dairy farm in the panhandle of Idaho. Shortly after that, in the early 1960's, the federal government mandated that all milk be pasteurized. By 1971, all of the dairies in my home county had closed; the cows had been moved to feedlot dairy farms. Our dairy was the last dairy to close up shop in 1971. The collapse of the family dairy farm happened all over the United States; more than 20 million family dairy farms went out of business.

Several changes occurred in the American diet because of required pasteurization of milk.

First, pasteurizing milk to very high temperatures denatures the native structure of omega-3 fats, which effectively destroys any potential benefits from this fatty acid. As a side note, cows' milk is also rich in many vitamins such as vitamin C. These vitamins are also destroyed in the pasteurization process.

Second, milk produced from cows raised on pasture land was rich in omega-3 fats. Shifting dairy cattle to feedlot farms led to a drop in the omega-3 content in the cows' milk. Feedlot-produced milk is much higher in **omega-6 fat (pro-inflammatory),** and much lower in **omega-3 fat (anti-inflammatory).** This is due to the type of fats found in the cattle feed. Cattle feeds usually contain vegetable oils rich in omega-6 fat derived from corn and soybeans.

Studies were conducted on herds of cattle in which one-half of the herd is fattened on pastureland while the other is fattened in the feedlot with omega-6 rich feed (Figure 2). The meat was then analyzed for the two groups. The grass-fed cattle had meat rich in omega-3 fats while the feedlot-fed cattle produced meat rich in omega-6 fats. The same kinds of results have now been found in chickens (and subsequently in their meat and eggs) and pigs (and their meat products).

Figure 2. The Effect of the Diet of Farm Animals on our Health.

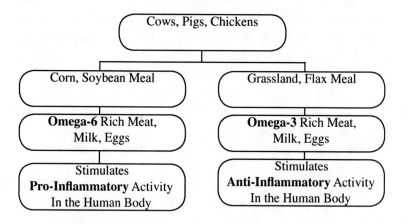

Third, about the same time, Americans stopped consuming cod liver oil. This oil was the other major source of omega-3 fat in our diet.

It had been known for many decades that cod liver oil would prevent rickets (a bone disease in children due to vitamin D deficiency) and night blindness (due to vitamin

A deficiency), and it was administered to children to prevent these disorders dating back to the 1800's. In the 1900's many jurisdictions in the United States required cod liver oil supplementation for children. I was required to take cod liver oil at school or have a document on file from my parents with the school nurse verifying cod liver oil consumption at home.

At the same time cod liver oil was discontinued in the American diet, the federal government mandated that pasteurized milk be vitamin fortified. Discontinuing cod liver oil in the American diet should have required omega-3 fatty acid supplementation as well as vitamin supplementation. However, omega-3 fat supplementation did not occur. In fairness to the Food and Drug Administration decision, the benefits of omega-3 fats had not been delineated yet.

With these two events, pasteurization of milk and the discontinuation of cod liver oil, the two primary sources of omega-3 fat (unpasteurized milk and fish oil) were eliminated from our diet. The shift to Trans (partially hydrogenated omega-6) fats ingestion and the drastic decrease in omega-3 fat intake led to a dramatic shift of omega-3: omega-6 from 1:1 to 1:20 ratio in the last century.

Date	Average Human Consumption of Fat	
	Omega-3/Omega-6 Ratio	Trans Fat %
1900	1-2/1	0%
1950	1/6	10%
1960	1/10	12%
1990	1/20	14%
2007	1/12-30	10%

One other interesting historical note was that shortly after the release in 1958 by Dr. Keys of the initial health warning concerning Trans fat use, the commercial vegetable oil industry began a campaign to malign saturated fat and cholesterol ingestion as the cause of heart disease. In one sense they were right. The consumption of beef had been a rich source of omega-3 fat. As cattle were shifted from small family farms to large commercial feedlots, the content of the polyunsaturated fat in the meat also shifted from omega-3 to omega-6 fats. So, indirectly the meat was now deleterious to our health. However, it was harmful because of the shift in the cattle's diet, not because of the saturated fat and cholesterol in the beef (see function of fat section below).

Function of Fat in the Human Body

The majority of the fat (also called lipid) ingested in the American diet is derived from triglycerides. Approximately two-thirds of these triglycerides are derived from animal fat and the rest from vegetable fat.

Fat makes up **numerous functions** in the body. These functions include

- **Electrical insulators around nerves**
- **Energy storage**
- **Biologic detergents**
- **Anchors for other molecules in the body**
- **Barriers between cells**
- **Regulators of immunity and inflammation**
- **Messenger molecules within a cell or between cells**
- **Hormones vital to health and reproduction**
- **Cushioning around organs**

Omega fatty acids are incorporated into the cell wall or membrane. In their native state they serve as electrical and moisture insulators for the cell. This is vitally important when cells are trying to send electrical transmissions to each other. After Trans omega-6 fats are incorporated into the cell wall rather than the native omega fats found in nature, these **artificial fats cause a "short-circuit" of the electrical current**. This can lead to all kinds of problems with the nervous system such as dementia, depression, attention deficit disorder, etc.

No one truly knows all the deleterious effects of Trans omega-6 fats on cell structure and function, but it is now quite clear that chronic ingestion of these fats leads to many medical conditions once rare or much less frequent than now seen in America.

Lipids, or fats, are hydrophobic molecules; that is, they are minimally soluble or completely insoluble in water. Fat is stored in the body primarily as triglyceride molecules. These molecules are composed of three fatty acids bound to a glycerol molecule. They are released from tissues in the body as a source of energy when stored glucose is depleted. Insoluble fat ingested during a meal is solubilized in the intestinal lumen by bile, the biologic detergent that allows fat to become water soluble. Once this occurs, the fat can then be absorbed across the intestinal lining into the bloodstream.

Cholesterol

I asked my wife one day what she believed is the **most important** way to **lower** your serum **cholesterol**. I gave her the following options:

1) Decrease your intake of cholesterol.
2) Decrease saturated fat intake.

3) Decrease Trans fat ingestion.
4) All of the above.
5) None of the above.

She replied that "4) all of the above" was the correct answer, and I asked her why? She then stated that she believed it because that is what she has learned from the media.

I then took an anonymous survey of several patients from my gastroenterology clinic. Their responses were uniformly the same as that of my wife.

It is fascinating to me that the myths about cholesterol abound in the American culture. The fact is that heart disease was a rare medical phenomenon until the introduction of Trans fats into the American diet. Families living on farms all across this country lived on diets high in saturated fats and cholesterol. Yet, they did not suffer from heart disease. No one had to check serum cholesterol levels, no one was taking a medication to lower their serum cholesterol level, and no one was dying of heart disease like that seen in today's environment. Yet, most doctors and the media do not see the connection.

Several studies have been performed that demonstrate serum cholesterol levels are minimally affected by dietary intake of cholesterol or saturated fats. Studies of the Masai and Samburu native tribes in Kenya, Africa are one example. These tribes live on a diet that is composed of raw cow's milk, cow's blood (when they slaughter their cows for meat), and meat from their cattle herds. Most adult males consume up to one-half pound of milk butterfat per day. The serum cholesterol of these Kenyan natives is one-half that of Americans, and **they do not suffer from heart disease at all**.

Initially, popular belief held that this lack of heart disease must be because the natives are genetically protected from elevated serum cholesterol and heart disease. Researchers decided to see if this was true so they followed the urbanization trail of the Masai people into Nairobi, Kenya. The natives in Nairobi had diversified their diets, and their serum cholesterol levels became elevated by over 25% compared with their native counterparts. If they were to move to America and consume our diet, their cholesterol levels would be indistinguishable from American levels. Numerous studies have revealed similar findings.

As can be seen from these people, a diet rich in cholesterol and saturated fats is not detrimental to their health, or ours. Their cattle are grass-fed cattle. The cattle produce meat and milk rich in omega-3 fat, "natural" Trans fat, cholesterol and saturated fat. This unadulterated combination of fats is beneficial to these African natives and to us as well. This is the way our farm fats were prior to the 1960's.

Finally, another proof that dietary cholesterol intake is not the issue, studies have shown that **complete elimination of all cholesterol in the diet** only **decreases** blood levels of **cholesterol by 2%.**

"Manufactured" Trans Fats

The **correct** answer to my question is **3) decrease Trans fat ingestion.** One of the disconcerting findings about Trans fat ingestion is that it raises serum levels of the "bad" cholesterol known as LDL cholesterol while it lowers the serum levels of the "good" cholesterol known as HDL cholesterol.

The "cholesterol-lowering" therapy directed by the health care industry is aimed at lowering LDL cholesterol. Billions of dollars are spent on medications annually in this country attempting to reduce the risk of heart disease by lowering this "bad" cholesterol.

The consistent findings that Trans fats cause "bad" cholesterol elevation (reported in numerous animal and human studies) has led to the recent systematic recommendation by numerous federal agencies and medical societies to markedly **reduce Trans fat ingestion**. In fact, the methodical elimination of Trans fats from foods prepared in New York City's 22,000 restaurants was mandated by the New York City Board of Health on July 1, 2007. It is sad to me that we have waited so long to react to Dr. Keys. In 1975 Finland eliminated all Trans fat from food production. Over the next 25 years they have seen a 50% reduction in heart disease in the general population.

The Food and Drug Administration (FDA) has a product labeling mandate to warn the American public about "Trans Fat" content in processed food. However, the federal government allows labels to read **"zero Trans fat"** even if there is a significant amount of this harmful fat remaining in the ingredients. The Food and Drug Administration requires the manufacturer to report the Trans fat content if a single serving size of a food product contains more than 500 mg of "partially hydrogenated fat.

I ask you: When does anyone ever eat just **"one serving"** of Ritz or other popular brand of crackers? One serving is **five crackers**. When I open a tube of those crackers to eat with my cheese and salami, I typically eat 16 crackers. That means that I just consumed nearly 1.5 grams of a toxic fat that leads to heart disease, cancer, and many other chronic inflammatory diseases. **1.5 grams;** in spite of the fact that the FDA allowed the manufacturer to say that I was eating **ZERO Trans fats per serving**. Boy, does that make me take a hard look at what I am now eating.

A patient in the office the other morning told me that she had a terrible "belly ache" a few evenings back after she had consumed an entire bag of "popular brand" potato chips that was cooked in partially hydrogenated fats. The "recommended serving" of this particular package was one-seventh of the bag. I think you get my point.

The important thing to realize is that the ingredient list of food labels is misleading. The **"partially hydrogenated** fat" is actually "**partially hydrogenated cottonseed oil**" or other "**Trans fat**" that causes chronic diseases in all of us.

If these are such dangerous fats that the New York City Board of Health is eliminating them from restaurants, why does the Federal government continue to allow not only significant consumption of the Trans fats, but deceptive food labeling as well? I do not know the answer to this question, nor can I find an answer in any of the literature I have studied.

"Natural" Trans Fats

A doctor in my gastroenterology practice questioned me the other day about Trans fats. "Dr. Greg" told me that he had heard that Trans fats are found in nature. This brings me to one of the most interesting aspects of fatty acid physiology that exists in all of nature and also takes us back to the farm and ruminant farm animals. What is a ruminant farm animal, you say? And what does that have to do with Trans fat?

Ruminants are even-toed, hoofed, usually horned, mammals such as cattle, sheep and goats. They digest their food in two steps. First, they eat raw food, typically grasses; then they regurgitate the partially-digested gastric contents and chew it up again. This process is called "chewing their cud." The animal's saliva is thoroughly mixed with the "cud," and the regurgitated matter is ground into very small particles. The animal then swallows the ground up "cud" where **bacteria ferment** the fibrous soup. The fermentation process produces numerous fatty acids that get incorporated into the animal's milk, muscles, and fat stores. Some of these fats are "natural" Trans fats known as **conjugated linoleic acids**. These are **"natural" Trans omega-6 fats**, as the name implies. As you will recall, linoleic acid is omega-6 fatty acid. When linoleic acid is found in plants and animals (other than ruminants) this fat occurs in a "non-Trans" form known as "Cis" or "curved" omega-6 fatty acid. Most of the "natural" Trans fats found in nature occur in animals involved with this bacteria-fermenting, rumination process.

Grassland-fed dairy cattle and their milk, beef, sheep, and goats and their milk products are **rich in conjugated linoleic acid** ("natural" omega-6 fats).

Very small quantities of "natural" Trans fats occur in all of the rest of nature, and they have little impact on human nutrition.

As you read earlier, manufactured, not natural, Trans omega-6 fats are quite detrimental to animal and human health. What is so fascinating to me is that these "natural" conjugated linoleic acids ("natural" Trans omega-6 fats) are not only harmless for animal or human consumption, they are actually quite beneficial. Numerous studies have been performed in the past decade concerning the beneficial properties of conjugated linoleic acids. The published benefits include:

- Reducing the risk for cancer formation
- Prevention of atherosclerosis
- Anti-diabetic effects, including improved insulin sensitivity
- Protective effect against inflammatory responses
- Improved body composition due to:
  o Decreased body fat mass
  o Increased lean body mass

The **cancer-reducing benefits of "natural" Trans fats** have been studied extensively in several animal models. Intestinal, breast and skin cancers are all reduced by the inclusion of these fats in the animal diet.

The reported mechanisms of the anti-cancer activity seen with ingestion of conjugated linoleic acids include:

a) **Reduction in cancer cell proliferation**
b) **Reduction in prostaglandin E2 production (which inhibits tumor creation)**
c) **Alteration of vitamin A metabolism.**

Total body wasting that is seen in cancer victims is also blocked by "natural" Trans fat ingestion.

Animal studies have shown that conjugated linoleic acids prevent atherosclerosis by reducing fat deposition and by blocking connective tissue development in the blood vessel. Both of these steps are well-recognized essential aspects of hardening of the arteries that leads to heart disease.

Rat and human studies also have demonstrated that these fats have an anti-diabetic effect. Improved insulin sensitivity and lowered fasting blood glucose levels occur with "natural" Trans fat ingestion.

Inflammation is a very important aspect of our physiology, as discussed in the previous chapter. Inflammation requires tight regulation, and unchecked inflammation can lead to significant damage to the body. Omega-3 fats are essential in manifesting this control, and the "natural" Trans omega-6 fats also play a role. The primary protective effect of these fats appears to be directed against the inflammatory factor called "tumor necrosis factor." The exact mechanism of tumor necrosis factor suppression by "natural" Trans fats has yet to be defined.

The final observations about conjugated linoleic fatty acids are the benefits seen in total body fat reduction and improved lean body mass. A specific fat in this family of "natural" Trans fats seems to be responsible for this: namely the trans-10, cis-12 form of the fatty acid molecule. While the mechanisms involved are still in discussion, reports reveal decreased synthesis and deposition of fat in the body, an increase in protein synthesis of muscle, and an increase in body energy expenditure (increased body metabolism rate).

These observations have led to the development and marketing of various formulations of "natural" Trans fats for weight reduction and muscle building. There is insufficient data concerning the safety of the "natural" Trans fats used in these marketed products, and you should consult your health care professional or qualified dietician before consuming them. It is important to note that some of the commercially produced conjugated linoleic acids are produced from vegetable oils rather than the "natural" Trans fats found in ruminants. No one knows whether these "manufactured" fats are equivalent to those found in nature.

Just as omega-3 and omega-6 fat content in cattle is dependent on food consumed by the animal, conjugated linoleic acid levels also vary in a similar manner. Cow's milk contains very high levels of omega-3 and conjugated linoleic acid fats when the animal grazes freely in pasture land. However, the conjugated linoleic acid levels decline substantially when cattle are confined to feedlots and fed grain meals. This same effect is found in the consumable meat from these ruminants. Cattle produced on the feedlots of America and Europe (fed primarily corn and other omega-6 fat-rich grains) have up to a threefold reduced level of conjugated linoleic acid compared to the pasture-fed cattle of New Zealand and Australia.

Doesn't it make you stop and think that perhaps we should get those 20 million family dairy farms back in business?

It makes you stop and wonder why we reduced the consumption of farm meat and other farm products. Was cholesterol and saturated fats found in these animals the problem or was it because of what the cattle were being fed that made their milk and meat products less healthy for us? It is obvious in hindsight that the latter is the case.

Saturated Fats

It is important to have a discussion about saturated fats. These fats have been misrepresented in the media, the federal government, and the American Heart Association almost as much as cholesterol. Saturated fats are found in many food sources from both plants and animals, such as coconut oil, cows' milk, and most meats (see Table 1). Saturated fats typically are shorter in length than the omega-3 and omega-6 fats. While they have been much maligned by the commercial vegetable oil industry and the medical establishment, the ridicule is misplaced. Many plants have as much saturated fat as animals, and they are the same kinds of saturated fats as found in animals. Does that make vegetables bad for us? I don't think so!!

These saturated fats typically function as an energy source, cell membranes of brain cells, antimicrobial protection in human breast milk for the baby, and lung surfactant (the substance that prevents the lung from collapsing). Ingestion of animal saturated fats has been advertised by the commercial vegetable oil industry as the cause of high cholesterol and heart disease in humans, and evidenced by my office survey, the public believes it.

I recently read an article in a reputable cardiology journal about the devastating affects of fats in heart health. The author paired Trans fats with saturated as the cause of heart disease in every sentence of his article. Yet, he gave no references to his paired association of these two fats to the cause of heart disease.

That is because there are no bibliographic references linking the two fats together as detrimental.

A few things about his conclusions are interesting to me. **First**, the saturated fats found in beef, pork, poultry, mutton or lamb are the same saturated fats as those found in plants. So, why are we educated not to eat meat that is high in saturated fat and to eat all the vegetables we want while they contain the same saturated fats?

Second, no scientific studies have ever linked saturated fat ingestion, per se, to elevated serum cholesterol or heart disease, let alone all the diseases that are now linked to the chronic ingestion of manufactured Trans omega-6 polyunsaturated fatty acids.

Third, these fats are essential to many body functions, and the body has the ability to convert and/or produce them as required as physiologic conditions demand.

Fourth, the federal government has now labeled olive oil a "heart healthy" food, and commercial growers are now able to label their products accordingly. What is interesting is that **the liver has the ability to transform saturated fat into olive oil** (oleic acid) as needed **and vice versa.** Logic says that:

1) **If oleic acid of olive oil is heart healthy**
2) **And saturated fats can be converted to oleic acid found in olive oil**
3) **Then saturated fats must also be heart healthy.**

The problem with consumption of animal products goes back to the total composition of animal fats. **The saturated fats found in animals are the same as that of plants,** but the composition of omega fats in the animal changes depending on the diet of the animal (as you know from previous discussion). This is the more accurate culprit, not the cholesterol and saturated fat in the meat and dairy products.

As mentioned earlier, if an animal has a **diet rich in omega-6 fats** (as is the case with feedlot cattle today in America), the cell walls of the meat become enriched with these omega-6 fats and depleted of "natural" Trans fats. We eat these fats, and they, in turn, are incorporated into our bodies' metabolism. **Together with: 1) the loss of our**

sources of omega-3 fat (unpasteurized milk, feedlot-fed farm animals, and cod liver oil), **2) the high level consumption of manufactured Trans omega-6 fat, and 3)** the **decrease in "natural" Trans fat from feedlot farming** helps us start to understand why our health in America has seriously suffered over the past one hundred years. It is time that we take control of our future health by changing our past dietary patterns. If not for ourselves, perhaps for future generations.

Pearls

- **Dietary ingestion of cholesterol and saturated fats in America <u>are not</u> the cause of inflammatory diseases**
- **Excess Omega-6 fat and "manufactured" Trans fats <u>are</u> the cause of inflammatory diseases in the USA**
- **Dietary Omega-3 fat deficiency is a major factor of inflammatory disease progression**
- **Loss of "Natural" Trans (CLA's) and Omega-3 fats from the American diet is due to commercial farming practices**

"Everything that lives and moves will be food for you. Just as I gave you the green plants, I now give you everything." Genesis 9:2

Chapter 6

Sources of Fats in Our Diet

In the previous chapter you learned about the specific kinds of fat found in nature that are relevant to what we consume on a daily basis. Before we get into the various disease processes that have been studied as they relate to fatty acids, it would be informative to educate you about the various sources of the fats in our diet. I do not have a quiz for you at the end of this chapter. Hopefully, it will serve more as a reference for you than as a challenge to your memory.

Cholesterol

Cholesterol is an essential component of the cell wall in animal tissues. It is also a building block for many hormones, scar tissue, some vitamins and antioxidants, and brain development early in life. While some of the cholesterol ingested in your diet contributes to your total body needs of cholesterol, the majority is synthesized by the liver. As demands go up, the liver responds by producing more cholesterol; if dietary intake increases, liver synthesis decreases accordingly. Be that as it may, dietary intake does not meet the daily requirements for the body's total body need for cholesterol. So, the liver fills in the gap.

Nearly all of our ingested cholesterol is derived from animal tissues. Only trace amounts are found in plant oils. When we consume cholesterol, it is not used as an energy source, nor is it stored in the body as fat. It is incorporated into the compartments of the body necessary for life as mentioned above. The cholesterol content of total animal fat is measured in milligrams of fat while other fats are measured in gram quantities. This amounts to one thousand times less than the other fatty constituents of animal fats (such as omega fats and saturated fats).

The richest sources of cholesterol in our diet are foods such as: eggs, breast milk, and milk butterfat from ruminant animals, meats from poultry, sheep, fish, cattle, wild game, and insects.

As a side note to cholesterol ingestion, vegetarians do not eat animal fat. Studies have shown that they have similar rates of heart disease as those who consume an omnivorous diet if the vegetarian also consumes "manufactured" Trans omega-6 fats from processed vegetable oils.

It is obvious that cholesterol is not the cause of heart disease in vegetarians because they do not consume animal-derived sources rich in cholesterol but still have heart disease if they consume a westernized diet rich in Trans and omega-6 fats.

Saturated Fats

Saturated fats are essential building blocks for our bodies. They are required for:

- The synthesis of some hormones
- Cell membrane strengthening
- Meeting energy demands for the body
- Signaling between cells
- Proper immune function
- Cancer prevention
- Cushioning around organs

Approximately 25% of the caloric intake in the diet should consist of saturated fats to help meet the needs of our bodies.

While all of these saturated fatty acids can be synthesized by the body, there are several naturally occurring saturated fats. These fats are the same whether they are found in plants or animals. For example, the palmitic acid found in milk butterfat is the same palmitic acid found in cottonseed oil. The capric acid found in butterfat of milk is the same as the capric acid found in coconuts. And so on.

The saturated fats occur as short-chain, medium-chain, and long-chain fatty acids, based on the length of the fat. This is an arbitrary division of the saturates as even research scientists do not always agree on which fat goes into which category. The longer the fatty acid, the higher its energy content, and the higher it's melting point from a solid to a liquefied form. Below is a list of the common saturated fats compiled with their common food sources.

Table 1. Saturated Fats and their Common Food Sources.

Saturated Fat Name	Common Food Source
1. Arachidic Acid	Peanuts
2. Behemic Acid	Peanuts
3. Butyric Acid	Butterfat of milk

4. Caproic Acid	Butterfat of milk, coconuts, palm kernel oil
5. Caprylic Acid	Coconuts, palm kernel oil, butterfat of milk
6. Capric Acid	Coconuts, palm kernel oil, butterfat of milk
7. Cetoleic Acid	Fish
8. Lauric Acid	Coconuts, palm kernel oil, butterfat of milk
9. Lignoceric Acid	Peanuts
10. Myristic Acid	Nutmeg, coconuts, palm kernel oil, butterfat of milk, animal fat
11. Palmitic Acid	Palm oil, cocoa butter, chicken fat, butterfat of milk, animal fat, cottonseed oil, seed oils
12. Stearic Acid	Cocoa butter, animal fat, butterfat of milk, chicken fat, seed oils

Monounsaturated Fat

Monounsaturated fats are long-chain fatty acids found both in plants and animals (see Table 2). The two most common forms found in foods that we consume are oleic acid (omega-9 fatty acid) and palmitoleic acid. They are liquid fats at room temperature.

Table 2. Natural Monounsaturated Fats

Monounsaturated Fat	Common Food Source
1. Cetoleic Acid	Fish oil
2. Gadoleic Acid	Rapeseed oil, fish oil
3. Gondoic Acid	Rapeseed oil, fish oil

4. Nervonic Acid	Animal brain, honesty seed oil
5. Oleic Acid	All animal and vegetable oils (see table 3)
6. Palmitoleic Acid	Marine animal oils, chicken fat, ruminant fat, pork lard, milk butterfat, olive oil
7. Vaccenic Acid	All animal/vegetable fats and oils

Oleic acid (omega-9 fatty acid) is the most common fat found in olive oil. Contrary to what you read on the http:// en.wikipedia.org/wiki.Saturated_fat website concerning oleic acid, it is also a major component of beef tallow and pork lard (see Table 3). It is the same oleic acid that is in the olive oil (named a heart healthy food by the United States Food and Drug Administration). The body metabolizes oleic acid into other essential saturated fats as is demanded by your body's needs.

Palmitoleic acid has natural anti-bacterial properties.

Numerous hydrogenated monounsaturated fats have been created by the commercial vegetable and marine oil industry. The physiologic value or possible toxicity of these fats to the human body is unknown. Just as it took nearly a century for the American public to be educated about the dangers of manufactured Trans omega-6 fats, it may take a long time for us to understand the biologic significance of these new "manufactured" oils. I will not discuss them further other than to remind you that there are known safe alternatives to the processed fats being forced on the American consumer.

Table 3. Common Food Sources of Oleic Acid (Omega-9 Fatty Acid).

Source of Oleic Acid	% of Total Fat Content
1. Almond Oil	61%
2. Avocado Oil	68%
3. Beef Tallow	48%
4. Butterfat of Milk	29%
5. Chicken Fat	36%
6. Egg	50%
8. Grape Seed Oil	16%
9. Hazelnut Oil	75%
10. Herring Oil	16%
11. Human Breast Milk	36%
12. Lamb Tallow	33%
13. Olive Oil	78%
14. Palm Oil	43%
15. Peanut Oil	45%
16. Pork Lard	44%
17. Rice Bran	42%
18. Rapeseed Oil (Canola – genetic hybrid)	56%
19. Safflower Oil (genetic hybrid)	74%
20. Sunflower Oil (genetic hybrid)	81%
21. Walnut Oil	23%

Polyunsaturated Fats

Polyunsaturated fatty acids are long-chain triglycerides found in green leafy vegetables, nuts, some grains and animals, especially marine fatty fishes. This group of fats contains the only known **essential fats** required for human existence. These include omega-6 fatty acid (linoleic acid) and omega-3 fatty acid (alpha linolenic acid). All other fats found in nature can be manufactured by the enzyme systems found in our bodies. Without these two essential fats, we would be unable to develop our brains, ward off infection, prevent cancer formation, prevent atherosclerosis, etc. While several polyunsaturated fatty acids are found in our food supply, they are not required by our bodies. They serve only as an energy source, much like the saturated and monounsaturated fats that we ingest.

Omega-6 fatty acid (linoleic acid) is the precursor fat for the production of pro-inflammatory molecules, blood clotting factors, and cell walls. They are found in highest concentrations in plant oils (see Table 4). Animals that consume high levels of omega-6 fat in their diet deposit this fat in their cell walls as part of the cell structural support. Our bodies must consume this oil on a daily basis to meet ongoing needs of maintenance and growth. The Food and Drug Administration recommends that we consume approximately 2-3% of our energy needs in the form of omega-6 fat. That means that we need between 4.5-6.5 grams of fat per day. That would be the equivalent of 2 teaspoonfuls of sunflower oil, one tablespoonful of corn oil, 2.5 tablespoonfuls of canola oil, or 5 tablespoonfuls of olive oil per day.

Table 4. Omega-6 Fatty Acid Sources in Our Diet

Dietary Source	Approximate % Omega-6 Fat
Almond Oil	30%
Avocado Oil	12%
Beef Tallow	2%
Borage Oil	38%
Chicken Fat	19%
Coconut Oil	2%
Corn Oil	57%
Cottonseed Oil	53%
Evening Primrose Oil	69%
Fatty Fish Oil	~1%
Flax Seed Oil	14%

Hazelnut Oil	15%
Lamb Tallow	4%
Milk Butterfat	3%
Olive Oil	10%
Palm Oil	10%
Palm Kernel Oil	2%
Peanut Oil	9%
Pork Lard	10%
Rapeseed Oil (canola)	19%
Rice Bran Oil	37%
Safflower Oil	78%
Sesame Oil	43%
Soy Bean Oil	53%
Sunflower Oil	68%
Walnut Oil	54%
Wheat Germ Oil	60%

Omega-3 fatty acid (alpha linolenic acid) is the other essential fat required to maintain a healthy body. The primary functions of alpha linolenic acid are to strengthen cell wall structure, produce anti-inflammatory precursors, and make blood anti-clotting factors.

The liver converts alpha linolenic acid (primary oil in flax seed oil) to the two fish oil omega-3 fats known as docosahexaenoic acid (DHA) and eicosopentanoic acid (EPA) in the presence of saturated fatty acids.

<u>Omega-3 Fatty Acids</u>

Alpha Linolenic Acid (parent omega-3 fat)
⇩
⇩
Liver Converting Enzymes
⇩
⇩
Docosahexaenoic acid (DHA) & Eicosopentanoic Acid (EPA)

One hundred years ago our diet contained relatively stable levels of omega-3 fatty acids. As covered in the previous chapter, until just recently, our intake of this essential fat plummeted almost into oblivion. Ingestion is making a comeback as the American public is starting to realize the importance of this fatty acid.

Our body needs to ingest approximately 2-3 grams of omega-3 fats per day. The richest sources of this **essential fat** are flax seed oil and fatty marine fish. We would need to ingest **approximately 1.5 to 2 teaspoonfuls of flax seed oil** (2 tablespoonfuls of ground flax) per day **or** up to **10 capsules of fish oil (1000 mg capsules) per day** of 200-300 mg of omega-3 fat per fish oil capsule. One 3.5 ounce serving of salmon has about one gram of omega-3 fat. As you can see, the best bang for the buck is flax seed oil, but it is good for the body to vary the sources of your oils.

The liquid and capsule preparations of the omega-3 fatty acids are quite safe and effective if they have been "cold" pressed rather than solvent extracted. Because these oils are vulnerable to deterioration by heat and sunlight they should be stored in a cool, dark place.

Table 5 shows the common sources of omega-3 fatty acids.

Table 5. Sources of Omega-3 Fatty Acids in our Diet.

Dietary Source	~ (%) Omega-3 Fat of Total Fat
Almond Oil	1%
Anchovy Oil	32%
Atlantic Salmon (farmed)	17%
Atlantic Salmon (wild)	27%
Avocado Oil	1%
Beef Tallow (Rendered Beef Fat)	1% (depends on beef's diet)
Catfish	15%
Caviar, Sturgeon	37%
Chicken Fat	1% (depends on chicken's diet)
Clams	15%
Cod Fish, Atlantic	27%
Cod Fish, Pacific	34%
Cod Liver Oil	14%
Crab, Blue	30%
Crab, Dungeness	31%
Crab, King	27%
Flax Seed Oil	55%
Grape Seed Oil	1%
Haddock	26%
Halibut	18%
Hemp Seed Oil	19%
Herring, Atlantic	18%
Herring, Pacific	12%
King Salmon	14%
Lard (Rendered Pig Fat)	1% (depends on pig's diet)
Lobster	13%
Mackerel	19%
Menhaden Oil	24%

Milk Butter Fat	1% (depends on cow's diet)
Mussels	19%
Octopus	15%
Oysters, Atlantic	25%
Oysters, Pacific	31%
Rice Bran Oil	1%
Salmon, King	14%
Salmon, Pink	30%
Salmon, Sockeye	15%
Sardines	37%
Sea Bass	30%
Sheep Tallow (Rendered Sheep Fat)	1% (depends on sheep's diet)
Shrimp, Large	29%
Shrimp, Small	29%
Snapper	23%
Sole	17%
Squid/Calamari	<1%
Trout, Rainbow	31%
Tuna Fish	Up to 30%
Turkey Fat	1% (depends on turkey's diet)
Walnut Oil	6%
Wheat Germ Oil	5%

The agricultural industry recently has become acutely aware of the importance of omega-3 fats in our diet. As mentioned earlier, the food ingested by the farm animal directly affects the amount of omega-3 fatty acid in the animal product. A local family farm is now selling chicken eggs that are enriched with omega-3 fats. Each egg contains 350 milligrams of omega-3 fat. Consuming two of these enriched eggs provides almost 30% of our daily requirement of omega-3 fats. Another example of food becoming enriched with omega-3 fats is grassland fed beef. This meat is rich in omega-3 fat whereas beef fed corn silage in a feedlot is rich in omega-6 fat.

Pearls

- **Our body needs 2-3 grams of omega-3 fat per day**
- **Flax seed oil and fish oil are the richest sources of omega-3 fatty acids**
- **Our diet contains excessive amounts of omega-6 fatty acids**

"Nevertheless, I will bring health and healing to it: I will heal my people and will let them enjoy abundant peace and security." Jeremiah 33:6

Chapter 7

Getting to the Heart of the Matter

How often do you get to see the effect of a diet deficient in an essential nutrient manifest itself before your very eyes? By the time I realized what was happening, the evidence of an essential fat deficiency spoke for itself. A long-time friend and colleague was making rounds at a local hospital and often would take the stairways rather than the elevator to keep himself in shape for ski season. He is an avid and excellent world class powder snow skier. One day not so long ago he became quite short of breath climbing the stairs and felt a little pressure under his breast bone. He did not think much about the initial event and figured that he must just be a little more out of shape because, after all, he had just eclipsed his 48th birthday.

This shortness of breath persisted for the next few weeks, but it finally dawned on him when he was skiing at Sun Valley, Idaho, during his annual rendezvous ski trip with his old high school buddies that perhaps he was suffering from heart pains. He was cruising down the beautiful powder slopes and, again the shortness of breath with exertion and heaviness in his chest area made him consider that he might be having angina (heart pain).

He began taking aspirin as a precaution, and, upon returning to work the next week, he made an appointment with a cardiologist. The heart specialist evaluated my dear friend and informed him that he was suffering from angina, or symptoms from a lack of oxygen getting to his heart muscle because of blocked heart arteries. My comrade and colleague then underwent heart catheterization, and three plastic tubes were placed in his heart vessels to keep them open. He also was started on several medications in an attempt to prevent future artery blockage.

Now for the rest of the story. My friend was one of those guys who never ate fish. His ancestry kept him from the native cardio protective diets of the Mediterranean, Middle East, Pacific Rim nations, or Scandinavia. He ate the "all-American" diet. I would attend medical conferences with him and noticed that his diet always consisted of pasta, poultry or beef. If we were dining at a medical banquet where fish was the main entrée, he would tell the host/hostess that he was allergic to fish so that they would bring him a special meal. He was not truly allergic to fish, but it was not a meal that he could bring himself to enjoy. As a result, during the past 25 years of our friendship and dining together, he has not eaten any appreciable omega-3 fats in his diet.

This scenario of premature heart disease is repeated daily somewhere in America. It was especially hard on me, however, as I contemplated the plight of my medical partner who is three years younger than me. Upon reflection about his health:

- He is not over-weight;
- He is a non-smoker;
- He is quite physically active;
- He does not have a family history of heart disease;
- He does not have high blood pressure;
- He does not have diabetes;
- He consumes a low-fat, low-cholesterol diet (wife Vera's orders); and
- He does not suffer from high cholesterol.

How is it that a person so young, with no identifiable cardiac risk factors, suffers from heart disease?

Could it be because he never was a fish eater?

Could it be that the great American low-fat, low-cholesterol diet did him in?

How important was his no fish diet as a contribution to his heart disease?

Could his heart disease have been prevented?

Is there anything that he can now do to prevent a second cardiac event?

So many questions! I will try to clarify in the remainder of this chapter the present knowledge about omega-3 fats as they relate to heart disease and my friend.

It is an amazing fact that in the United States approximately 3,000 people suffer a heart attack every day. The National Institutes of Health in Bethesda, Maryland, claims that 1.25 million Americans have a cardiac event **annually**. That means that 1 in 217 people will have a heart attack this year **and** next year **and** the year after that. Is there no way to reduce the risk of heart disease in America?

Primary Prevention

In the late 1970's it was first learned and published that Greenland Eskimos have a low incidence of heart disease. These people eat a diet rich in fatty marine food of the north Atlantic (fish, seals, whales). Even though they were consuming a high-cholesterol, high-fat diet (a diet that American agencies such as the Food and Drug Administration and the American Heart Association have been advocating against for the past 40 years), the Eskimos were not dying from heart disease. While heart disease accounted for 28.5% of all deaths in America, it constituted only 3.5% of all deaths among the Greenland population.

Initially, research scientists thought that the Eskimos were genetically protected from heart disease. When it was discovered that the Greenland Eskimos who had migrated to Denmark assumed the same increased incidence of heart disease of the Danes, this hypothesis went by the wayside. The scientists concluded that a diet rich in fatty marine life was protecting the Eskimos from heart disease.

What is sad is that, as these Eskimos have now begun eating a more "industrialized" diet of Trans omega-6 fats, their rate of heart disease has risen to that of the rest of us.

A short time after the Greenland observation was reported, the results were published of a prospective 20-year study begun in 1960 in the Netherlands. This study demonstrated a 50% reduction in death from heart disease among Dutch men who ate as little as **one ounce of fresh fish per day** compared to those who ate no fish at all. The conclusion was that **not eating fish is a risk factor for the development of heart disease**.

It is amazing to me that even though I took four semesters of biochemistry in college and medical school, completed Internal Medicine training studying the risks of heart disease, and studied nutrition in Gastroenterology fellowship, I never was educated about the importance of these astounding studies. More importantly, I was never educated about omega-3 fats. In all of my biochemistry and medical education I never was taught about the importance of omega-3 fats, only omega-6 fats. One without the other is deadly. **Both omega-6 and omega-3 fats are needed to keep the body healthy.** As I have studied and learned on my own, I have grown to appreciate the vital importance of omega-3 fats in protecting the heart as well as the rest of the body.

Let us return to the Greenland Eskimo story for a moment. Scientists were perplexed with other findings in the study. The Eskimos' blood was analyzed and found to be low in fat content. The serum cholesterol and triglyceride levels were far below that of the American population. The paradox of consuming a high-fat diet and having low blood levels of fat made no sense to the researchers.

The aftermath of this paradox led to a number of studies aimed at lowering cholesterol in one camp, and omega-3 fat supplementation in the other in an attempt to lower heart disease and its associated mortality.

A little more background is necessary before the paradox can be fully appreciated. In the 1950's, Dr. Ancel Keys from the University of Minnesota led a campaign to improve the American diet in an attempt to reduce the ravages of heart disease in America. He published a paper in 1953 that suggested that a high-fat, high-cholesterol diet was associated with cardiac death rates around the world, especially in the United States.

This publication stimulated the media and organized medicine to launch a nationwide campaign aimed at attempting to reduce heart disease by lowering cholesterol and saturated fat in the American diet. The concept was that a diet high in cholesterol and saturated fat caused high blood cholesterol. Chronic elevated cholesterol levels would then build up plaques of cholesterol in blood vessels. The cholesterol would slowly clog the blood vessels and heart disease would develop.

This led to a push by the agribusiness and pharmaceutical industry to develop products (Trans fats, medications) that would lower intake of saturated fats and cholesterol, and lower serum cholesterol. Trans fats were developed by the food industry as an answer to improve polyunsaturated fats. The process converts the liquefied form of the polyunsaturated fat (found in oils such as corn, soybean, cottonseed, and sunflower oil) into a solid fat while still maintaining their unsaturated state.

Using the polyunsaturated liquid oils rather than butter and lard (saturated fats thought to be bad) created a problem in the kitchen and at the dinner table. Cooking with the oil was problematic. It burnt easily and could not be spread on bread in a liquid state. The Trans fat rearrangement solved the problem by causing the polyunsaturated liquid to become solid while maintaining the polyunsaturated state.

Trans fats were quickly incorporated into the great American diet. Shortly thereafter studies concerning the lack of safety of Trans fats quickly emerged. Several investigations demonstrated the association of Trans fat ingestion with increased risk of cancer and heart disease.

By 1958 Dr. Keys and other scientists attempted to notify the food industry and the American government of the dangers of chronic Trans fat ingestion. The edible vegetable oil industry promptly brought attacks on saturated fat and cholesterol (meat, saturated fats such as palm oil, and dairy products) as the cause of cancer and heart disease. This caused significant economic damage to the beef and dairy industry while the ravages of Trans fats silently took their toll on the health of the American public. It was not until 2005, almost 50 years after Dr. Keys' attempted to notify the government and the public of Trans fat dangers in a published paper, that the Food and Drug Administration

(FDA) advised the American public of the potential dangers of Trans fats. The FDA mandated the labeling of Trans fats on all food products in that year. Subsequently, some of the Trans fats have been removed from the grocery store shelves; however, many of these fats are being hidden by "fine print" labeling. In my estimation, this removal is driven more by fear of class action lawsuits rather than health detriments, because the conclusion of their unsafe consumption has been known for over 50 years.

Two events which took place in America in the early years of the 1960's complicate the saturated fat saga.

First, the FDA mandated the pasteurization of all milk products consumed in the United States. This process protected the American public from potential tuberculosis infections transmitted from cows' milk (a problem that did not even exist because the FDA had already implemented adequate testing and treatment programs for cattle in the United States). At the same time, this process destroyed the natural omega-3 fats found in the milk.

Second, cod liver oil was removed from the American diet. Until that time, unpasteurized milk, butter and cod liver oil had been the mainstay of omega-3 fat ingestion in the Western diet. With the pasteurization process, the FDA mandated fortification of milk with vitamins A and D (found in high concentrations in cod liver oil). Supplementing the diet with cod liver oil was no longer recommended by the FDA.

Let us now return to the omega-3 heart disease prevention story. Because the American diet had become saturated with Trans fats and devoid of any significant amounts of omega-3 fats, several studies trying to sort out the Greenland and Dutch studies led to contradictory findings. So no definitive conclusions could be reached for the next few decades.

In spite of confusion in these studies and a strong resistance by the edible plant oil industry, the truth slowly

By the mid-1990's, several prospective, randomized trials using various sources of omega-3 fat supplements demonstrated a reduction in the incidence of heart disease. Additionally, large population-based studies revealed that consuming a diet rich in either plant or marine omega-3 fats reduced premature heart disease. By 1996 the American Heart Association (AHA) produced its *Science Advisory to the American Public* about the benefits of omega-3 fatty acids on cardiovascular disease. And, in 2002 the AHA published recommendations for omega-3 fatty acid intake (see Table 1 below).

Table 1. Summary of Recommendations for Omega-3 Fatty Acid Intake Published by the American Heart Association

Population	Recommendation
Patients without heart disease	Eat a variety of fish at least twice a week. This includes oils and foods rich in alpha-linolenic acid (flax, soy, canola, walnuts)
Patients with documented heart disease	Consume about 1 gram of EPA[1] +DHA[2] /day, preferably from fatty fish. EPA + DHA in capsule form could be considered in consultation with the physician.

| Patients who need to lower serum triglycerides | 2 to 4 grams of EPA + DHA/day provided as capsules under a physician's care. |

[1]EPA = Eicosapentaenoic Acid
[2]DHA =Docosahexaenoic Acid

Much is still to be learned about omega-3 fats as they relate to heart disease. Studies to date demonstrate a reduction in heart disease risk in several ways following dietary omega-3 fat supplementation. Published data reveal:

- **Decrease in sudden death** from a heart attack
- **Decrease in cholesterol plaque build-up** in blood vessels
- **Decreased risk of abnormal heart rhythms**
- **Decrease in serum triglyceride levels**
- Slight **improvement in blood pressure**
- **Decrease in non-fatal heart attacks**
- **Decrease in total mortality** *(all causes)*

Despite the controversy surrounding the use of omega-3 fat supplementation to reduce the risk of heart disease, the American Heart Association (AHA) is now recommending some form of dietary modification to include omega-3's. Additionally, in 2005 the Food and Drug Administration modified the "food pyramid" to recommend ingesting foods or supplements rich in omega-3 fats on a regular basis.

Treatment/Secondary Prevention

It would seem intuitive that consuming a diet rich in omega-3 fats would be of benefit once a person has developed heart disease. As can be seen from the AHA guidelines (Table 1) it is now recommended that patients with documented heart disease should be ingesting a diet rich in omega-3 fats daily. This recommendation is based on several studies that have revealed a reduction in blood vessel plaque build-up, recurrent heart attack, sudden death, heart attack deaths, nonfatal heart attack, and total mortality from all causes. These studies have included fish, fish oil and plant-based oil supplementation. There is still controversy concerning the ideal dose for secondary prevention of heart disease. Prospective studies suggest a dose of 0.5 to 1.8 grams of fish or fish oil supplements or 1.5 to 3 grams of plant omega-3 fat per day. More definitive research is needed to better define the appropriate doses and the best type of omega-3 supplementation.

In Summary

As can be seen from the information presented, heart disease and its severe consequences are having a devastating impact on the American culture. As for my friend and colleague, he and I will never know whether his premature heart disease could have been prevented. It is quite clear that he lived on a diet rich in Trans fats, and he almost never consumed omega-3 fats. While the American diet probably was a contributing factor, none of us have a crystal ball. Since the plastic tubes were placed in his heart arteries, he has started taking omega-3 oil daily, he avoids all Trans fats, and he has not had any further chest pains for the past three years. His most recent heart checkup was normal.

Pearls

- **Heart disease is caused by the ingestion of Trans fats**
- **Omega-3 fats reduce the risk of heart disease**
- **Cholesterol and saturated fats do not cause heart disease**

"Everything is permissible – but not everything is beneficial." 1 Corinthians 10:23

Chapter 8

The Cancer-Fat Connection

Three receptionists and one licensed practical nurse who have worked in my gastroenterology office over the past five years have developed breast cancer. Additionally, another nurse is undergoing continued treatments for lymphoma (a lymph gland cancer). These are just the employees in my practice about whom I personally know. I also have a cousin fighting for her life because of lymphoma, and my wife has a family member who has been stricken with lymphoma. When I was a medical student 30 years ago, it was a rare event to see a patient afflicted with lymphoma. In our medical practice today, a gastrointestinal cancer is diagnosed by me or one of my partners nearly every single day.

Nearly everyone in America today personally knows someone who in the past few years has been afflicted with and/or died from some form of malignancy.

Why is it that America represents 5% of the world's population and yet accounts for 14.5% of the cancers? Cancer accounts for 23% of all deaths is the United States, second only to heart disease.

Additionally, when immigrants who have a much lower cancer risk than Americans assimilate the American diet rather than consuming their native diets after they come to America, their cancer risks mimic people who have been in the United States for generations. Americans have a shorter life expectancy than many of the other industrialized nations in the world.

An astonishing 1.45 million Americans are diagnosed with cancer annually, and 560,000 people will die from some form of cancer. That represents over **1,500 cancer-related deaths each day.** That means **1,500** today, another **1,500** tomorrow, and another **1,500** every day in the foreseeable future. Why?

As can be seen by the recent warnings by the federal government, Trans fats now have been linked to the formation of cancer. Accordingly, an announcement by the Food and Drug Administration in November 2005 mandated that all food labels divulge the content of Trans fats beginning January 1, 2006. Trans fats are vegetable oils that have been chemically altered to improve shelf life, customer appeal and cooking qualities. They are found predominately in margarines and shortenings.

Even with the new labeling requirements, the federal government allowed the manufacturers to conceal Trans fats under the heading of "partially hydrogenated oils." The reason for this is unclear to me at the time of this writing. Regardless, numerous studies have revealed that Trans fats are promoters of cancer more than the other fats, for the reasons below.

But there is more to the story than the impetus for cancer formation by Trans fats. When I began my research for this book, I was astonished to discover the importance of **omega-3 fatty acids in the prevention of cancer**. What emerged from the dozens of articles that I reviewed concerning omega-3 fats and cancer was that nearly every paper suggested that diets rich in these oils reduce the risk of cancer formation. With the exception of apparently unexplained contradictory data concerning prostate cancer and certain forms of omega-3 fat ingestion, all studies were in agreement that cancer risk is inversely proportional to omega-3 fat consumption; that is, **the more omega-3 oil ingested, the lower the cancer risk.**

As I tried to dissect the literature concerning this very complicated subject, I became confused. It has always been realized that the body needs linoleic acid (omega-6 fatty acid) to maintain health. As the knowledge and understanding of fat metabolism grew during the later part of the 20th century, it became abundantly clear that the other essential fatty acid for human well-being was alpha-linolenic acid (omega-3 fatty acid). If the body has too much omega-6 fat and not enough omega-3 to counteract the former's inflammatory effects on the body, the inflammation will go unchecked.

Chronic inflammation of the vascular system leads to heart and blood vessel disease.

Chronic inflammation of the breast (fibrocystic breasts) leads to breast cancer.

Chronic inflammation of joints leads to arthritis.

Chronic inflammation of the colon (colitis) leads to colon cancer.

Get the picture? **Omega-3 fatty acids are essential in activating <u>anti-inflammatory</u> metabolic pathways in the entire body.**

Omega-3 fats counter-balance omega-6 fats to keep inflammation (and in turn, cancer) in check. While Trans fats are inciting cancer formation in the body, a deficiency of omega-3 fat (in the presence of an excess of omega-6 and Trans fat in the American diet) is leading to a cancer incidence that is the highest in the world.

As was stated in an earlier chapter, omega-6 oil is abundant in corn, soy, cottonseed, and safflower oil. These oils were the mainstay of the American diet for over 50 years. Additionally, lard and butter were supplanted by shortening and margarine following the development of Trans fats. Omega-3 oil is abundant in fish, flax and canola oil. The Food and Agriculture Organization of the United Nations in a joint statement with the World Health Organization (FAO/WHO) published their *"Experts' Recommendations"* on fats and oils in human nutrition in 1994. In their report they stated:

> "High intake of Trans fatty acids is undesirable, but it is not yet certain whether the use of Trans or saturated fatty acids is preferable where such fatty acids are required in formulation of food products."

As mentioned in the heart chapter, information concerning the deleterious effects of Trans fats was provided to the Food and Drug Administration in 1958. In January 2006, the American public was officially notified of the dangers of Trans fat consumption in the form of **mandatory food labeling**. During this 12-year hiatus from the FAO/WHO warning, and 48-year differential from the FDA insight, I wonder how many people have suffered or died since the early 1960's from the ravages of cancer from continued consumption of Trans fats without appreciable omega-3 fat consumption.

While the Trans fat saga was being played out, the omega story also takes a twist. FAO/WHO made the following recommendations in the same 1994 report:

> "The ratio of linoleic to alpha-linoleic acid (omega-6 to omega-3) should be between 5:1 and 10:1."

What perplexes me about this recommendation is that the higher the omega-6 to omega-3 fatty acid ratio in the diet, the higher the cancer risk. This has been reported in animal models as well in human observations. Genetic studies in research animal models demonstrate that diets supplemented with **omega-3 fatty acids reduce the incidence of breast cancer** by several mechanisms.

Without giving a dissertation about cancer genetics, let me state simply that cancer can be stopped by tumor suppressor genes coded into our DNA. **Omega-3 fats suppress the expression of two different cancer genes that lead to the formation of breast cancer.** Studies also show that the higher the omega-3 to omega-6 ratio in the diet, the lower the cancer risk in animals:

- **Cancer incidence is reduced by at least 30%**
- **Tumor growth rate is suppressed**
- **Animal life with cancer is prolonged**
- **Tumor mass size is reduced**
- **Cancer-induced anorexia and cachexia are markedly reduced**

The earlier and longer the omega-3 fatty acids are introduced to the animal before cancers are introduced into the animal, the better the results against the ravages of cancer. Improved cancer outcome in animal models has been seen with lung, colon, mammary and prostate cancers.

It is interesting to note that these are the most common cancers ravaging America.

Human data also agree with the research animal studies. Epidemiologic investigations reveal that diets rich in omega-3 fatty acids reduce the risk of cancer.

The only data that I can find that contradicts this is related to prostate cancer. Even with prostate cancer, some forms of omega-3 fats are protective in epidemiologic studies. All prospective studies to date have shown reduced prostate cancer risk.

Population-based retrospective epidemiologic data can be hard to interpret because of so many variables, for which none have been controlled. Data now exists demonstrating the benefits of omega-3 fat in the prevention of colon, breast and prostate cancer as well as lymphoma.

Diets enhanced with omega-3 oils also reduce tumor growth and metastatic spread in patients with cancer. Tumor marker expression also decreases in cancer subjects with omega-3 fat supplemented diets. Additionally, cancer treatment with chemotherapy and radiation therapy is improved when the diet is enhanced with omega-3 fats. Other research has revealed that cancer-related cachexia is suppressed and quality of life is improved with omega-3 supplementation.

I have reviewed numerous studies covering many years of research gathered from animal and human data. **Cancer risk increases with the ingestion of Trans fats and with a diet with a high omega-6 to omega-3 fat ratio.**

The ingestion of saturated fats and cholesterol seem to be cancer neutral. Most importantly, omega-3 fats as well as diets with high omega-3 to omega-6 fat ratios are protective against the devastation of cancer.

You may recall in Chapter 5, *Fundamentals of Fats*, that natural Trans fats (conjugated linoleic acids), are also protective against cancer formation. I would refer you back to that chapter rather than recapitulate it here.

While it was too late for me to have an impact in preventing the cancers from which my employees suffered, I can encourage everyone with whom I come into contact with to stop eating Trans fats and start increasing omega-3 fats in their diets.

Maybe, just maybe, someone will not have to become one of those **1,500** cancer victims tomorrow or **1,500** the next day. . . .

Pearls

- The primary cause of cancer in America is the chronic ingestion of Trans fats
- Omega-3 fat supplementation reduces your risk of cancer
- Decreasing the omega-6 to omega-3 fat ratio in your diet will reduce your risk of developing cancer

*"My weary nights are filled with pain as though
something were relentlessly gnawing at my bones."
Job 30:17*

Chapter 9

What Fat Is in Your Bone?

Arthritis

After covering the biggest killers in the United States in the previous two chapters (heart disease and cancer), I would now like to move on to one of the most debilitating health problems that we face today.

Arthritis affects nearly all Americans during the aging process. The deformity, pain and suffering can be next to unbearable. Since I started educating patients about the importance of omega-3 fat in their diet, I could write a book of anecdotes about reduced pain and suffering shared with me daily by my patients. By the end of this chapter, hopefully you will have a better appreciation about the benefit of taking omega-3 fats for your joint health as well as your heart and cancer-prone organs.

I want to take you back to the Greenland Eskimos for a moment. As you might recall from Chapter 6, these natives had no appreciable heart disease. What also is amazing is that they did not suffer from arthritis either. Because heart disease often is fatal, whereas arthritis rarely leads to death, little time has been spent investigating this aspect of the Eskimos' health. The story, in retrospect, now is clear.

Joint disease comes in many forms. The most common arthritis is osteoarthritis. Other forms of arthritis include rheumatoid arthritis, gouty arthritis, arthritis related to inflammatory bowel disease (Crohn's disease and ulcerative colitis), juvenile rheumatoid arthritis, and others.

The common denominator in arthritis is inflammation. Some of these diseases are associated with immune deregulation; that is, the immune system is out of balance. The immune system actually develops the ability to attack the body and various organs within it. In this case, it is the bones and joints.

Some individuals suffer from inflammatory diseases of the intestines that can have associated joint inflammation. Others may suffer from inherited metabolism disorders, such as gout, where uric acid crystals can get deposited in tissues (including joints), leading to severe inflammation.

My sister had been suffering for years from psoriatic arthritis and inflammation of her joints and fingernail beds. She had been treating it with ibuprofen for years in an attempt to reduce the pain and swelling. One day she asked me if I had any suggestions to help with her problem. I asked her if she was supplementing her diet with omega-3 fats. Of course, the answer was, "No." With my prompting, she began taking flax seed oil and decreased her Trans and omega-6 fat ingestion. Within several weeks, her hands and fingernails were causing her far less discomfort. Within a few months her fingernail beds returned to a normal appearance for the first time in her memory. She continues to take her omega-3 fatty acid supplements and has remained pain free for the past several years. Deformities in her fingernail beds have not returned.

Why is it that the Greenland Eskimos and my sister have their stories to tell, yet the controversy about omega-3 supplementation rages on? As recently as January 2007 a nutritional review article discussing joint health did not even suggest omega-3 fatty acid supplementation in the summary section of the manuscript. Yet, a meta-analysis (a systematic review paper of all pertinent published research trials related to a specific subject) published in May 2007 was quite revealing in its evaluation of the beneficial effects of omega-3 fatty acid supplementation for patients suffering from inflammatory joint pain. The analysis reviewed 17 randomized, controlled studies assessing the pain relief benefits of omega-3 fats and found that 3 to 4 four months of these supplements reduced:

- **morning stiffness**
- **the number of tender joints**
- **the amount of anti-inflammatory medication required for symptom control**

The conclusion of this manuscript was that omega-3 fatty acids are "an attractive adjunctive treatment for joint pain associated with rheumatoid arthritis, inflammatory bowel disease and dysmenorrhea."

What is also interesting to me beyond the lack of agreement between these two papers is that the "joint health" article did not recommend reduction of omega-6 fats or Trans fats. The importance here is that both of these fats stimulate the pro-inflammatory mediators of the body while omega-3 fats promote the anti-inflammatory substrates (see Chapter 4 to refresh your memory). It would seem that these considerations would be essential to a review article on "nutritional consideration in joint health."

Several mechanisms relevant to the biochemical effects of omega-3 fatty acids now have been determined to be important in reducing inflammation, and in turn pain associated with joint disease. These fats suppress the production of some inflammatory mediators such as tumor necrosis factor alpha (TNF-a). Many very expensive medications have been developed and are now on the market to suppress TNF-a, such as Embril, Humira, Rituxan, and Remicade. These medications often are used in the treatment of severe arthritic conditions. They all have many potential dangerous side effects.

Would these individuals have reached the point of needing one of these medications if they had not been deficient in omega-3 fatty acids or not had an excess of omega-6/Trans fats in their bodies from the outset?

These same fats also suppress the pro-inflammatory pathways that are suppressed by corticosteroids (such as prednisone) and non-steroidal anti-inflammatory medications (such as aspirin, ibuprofen, naproxen, etc.). The problem is that even though one may supplement his or her diet with omega-3 fatty acids, the benefits may be diminished with the ingestion of Trans fats and omega-6 fats. Omega-6 fats compete with the same enzyme pathways and can overwhelm the benefits of the omega-3 fat supplementation if omega-6 fat ingestion is excessive. Remember Chapter 6, where I mentioned that the government recommendations of omega-6 to omega-3 ratio in the diet should be between 5:1 and 10:1. Data clearly show that the anti-inflammatory benefits of omega-3 fats should place that ratio around 2:1 to 1:1 (the ratio seen in America only 100 years ago), maybe even less. To date, this is a hotly debated subject without resolution in sight.

The lack of control of omega-6 fat intake in the diet in some studies probably accounts for the lackluster benefit in joint relief that is otherwise seen in other studies supplementing with omega-3 fatty acids while also reducing omega-6 fat intake.

Osteoporosis

As we have seen, the anti-inflammatory effects of omega-3 fatty acids can improve the quality of life for those afflicted with inflammatory bone joint disease. What about the rest of our bones? What about the bone itself? The most common metabolic bone disease crippling America is osteoporosis. **This bone-wasting disease affects approximately 1 in 10 Americans; that is, 28 million individuals.** If you realize that it is a disease that typically does not affect young adults, then the incidence of the disease is much higher than the one in ten cited.

I recently interviewed a patient who has had two hips and one knee replaced because of osteoporosis. He is only 61 years old presently, which means that he was in his 50's when his joints were replaced.

How is it that so many Americans are so diseased at such a young age? Forty percent of women and 13% of men will develop one or more osteoporosis-induced bone fractures in their lifetime. More than 1.5 million people develop a new osteoporotic bone fracture each year (4,110 people each day of the year). This translates to 250,000 hip, 250,000 wrist and 500,000 vertebral spine fractures each year. The "baby boomer" generation is rapidly approaching the age of increased susceptibility for osteoporosis. It is even more disconcerting that projections are anticipated to rise exponentially in the next couple of decades for:

- the number of those anticipated to become afflicted with osteoporosis;
- osteoporosis-induced bone fractures;
- the increased mortality associated due to the loss of ambulation after a hip fracture (12-24% mortality in women and 30% mortality in men in the first year after a hip fracture); and

- increased demands on assisted living and nursing homes (50% of individuals afflicted require ambulatory assistance after a fracture).

Why are we seeing so much osteoporosis in so many aging Americans? We have been taught that the risk factors for developing osteoporosis, and subsequent bone fractures, include:

- low dietary calcium and vitamin D intake,
- eating disorders,
- low testosterone levels in men,
- premenopausal estrogen deficiency in women,
- excessive alcohol intake,
- physical inactivity,
- lack of sunlight exposure,
- cigarette smoking,
- low body weight,
- excess coffee, tea and cola intake, and
- rapid weight loss.

Diseases such as Crohn's disease (an inflammatory intestinal disorder), sex hormone deficient states (for both males and females), and thyroid, parathyroid and adrenal gland disorders have also been associated with osteoporosis.

Finally, taking medications such as prednisone are associated with this bone disorder. It is interesting that none of the leading textbooks in bone disease (rheumatology), endocrinology or internal medicine makes **any** mention of the **importance of omega-3 fatty acids in the prevention of osteoporosis**.

If you recall from the first chapter discussing essential fatty acid deficiency, it was recognized in the 1800's in England that cod liver oil prevented bone disease. It was subsequently learned that cod liver oil is rich in vitamin D, an essential component of bone development. What was not discovered until over a century later was that cod liver oil is also a good source of omega-3 fatty acid. Data now reveal that animals fed a diet deficient in essential fatty acids develop severe osteoporosis. This bone disease is also coupled with kidney and arterial blood vessel calcification. Further delineation of these findings shows that deficiency of omega-3 fatty acids is responsible. Animal studies have been performed creating omega-3 fat deficiency and subsequent osteoporosis. When the animals are then supplemented with omega-3 fatty acids, their bones developed accelerated normalization of bone formation.

Essential fatty acids have now been shown to increase calcium absorption in the intestine (by enhanced vitamin D effects), reduce calcium excretion in the urine (calcium wasting), increase calcium deposition in the bone, and increase bone strength. If you recall from the chapter discussing the anti-inflammatory effects of omega-3 fatty acids (Chapter 4), these fats reduce or block the effects of the pro-inflammatory substances produced by omega-6 fats/Trans fats. Much more insight now exists in animal and human studies that these pro-inflammatory factors cause osteoporosis by stimulating bone to dissolve. Omega-3 fats block this process. A study published in January 2007 concluded that a diet rich in walnuts and flaxseed oil "may have a protective effect on bone metabolism via a decrease in bone dissolution in the presence of consistent levels of bone formation."

It is likely that most of the risk factors associated with osteoporosis are valid. What is exciting to me is that as our understanding of essential fatty acids grows, maybe **we can have a major impact on metabolic bone disease just by:**

- **increasing omega-3 fats in our diet while**
- **eliminating Trans fats and**
- **decreasing omega-6 fat intake.**

Once these animal and human studies are validated and better elucidated, this could potentially have an enormous impact on the reduction of metabolic bone disease in America.

In the meantime, the current data (now spanning over a decade of research) clearly convince me that I need to stay on a diet rich in omega-3 fatty acids and low in omega-6/Trans fats to better protect my joints and bones.

Pearls

- **Omega-3 fats supplementation can reduce metabolic bone disease**
- **Omega-3 fat supplementation improves the quality of life in patients suffering from inflammatory bone disease**
- **Osteoporosis can be reversed with the decrease of omega-6 fats, elimination of Trans fats, and supplementation of omega-3 fat.**

"The Lord will guide you continually, watering
your life when you are dry and keeping you
healthy." Isaiah 58:11

Chapter 10

The Lipid Is in the Liver

N ever a day goes by in my gastroenterology clinic that
I do not see a new patient with a fatty (lipid) liver.
The official medical name for fatty liver disease is non-alcoholic fatty liver disease (NAFLD). NAFLD is now the most
common form of liver disease in America and affects nearly
two percent of the population. Have you ever had a relative
who died of cirrhosis of the liver only to be told by your
physician that he/she must have been a "closet alcoholic?"
Granted, alcohol abuse can lead to fatty liver and cirrhosis,
but NAFLD is frequently the cause of liver disease in the
absence of alcohol abuse.

Why are so many people in the United States developing
NAFLD? I rarely saw this disorder when I was a young
physician 25 years ago. Today I have dozens of patients on
treatment for this disorder.

Clues about this disorder go back to research findings
first reported in the 1920's. As pointed out in the chapter on
essential fatty acid deficiency (Chapter 1), placing animals

on a diet devoid of any fat causes fatty liver disease that is reversible upon refeeding the animals fats. An understanding of the two essential fatty acids (omega-3 and omega-6) was not understood at that time. Further insight into the understanding of fatty liver formation occurred when intravenous nutritional therapy was being developed in the 1970's and 1980's. The early formulas did not include fat. People developed abnormal liver chemistries and fatty liver within days of being on a fat-free intravenous diet. Evolution of these intravenous feeding formulas now includes fatty acid supplementation to prevent NAFLD.

Ten years ago I started placing patients on flaxseed oil to see if I could reduce the liver chemistries and liver damage in patients suffering from NAFLD. I found that many patients had a complete reversal of their chemistries and damage over the next few years. I presented my data at the annual meeting of the American College of Gastroenterology in the fall of 2006. Few physicians took note of the findings.

While I have been routinely teased and/or ridiculed by some of my partners, my patients were slowly reversing the damage in their livers. Not all got better, though. Searching the literature in preparation for writing this book has given me better insight about the poor responders. I failed to counsel these patients about decreasing their omega-6/Trans fat intake at the same time. I am now incorporating these recommendations into their health plan. It will be curious to see if this additional intervention will correct the NAFLD in the poor responders.

An editorial in the April 2007 Journal *"Hepatology"* (liver disease) commented on the importance of omega-3 fatty acids and liver disease: "Fish oil has become the hot topic in nutrition and health care in general over the past few years. With any therapy that receives inordinate attention from the lay press, though, scientists and health care providers must approach this issue with a healthy dose of professional skepticism." However, the articles go on to state that: "contrary to previous 'fads,' the benefits of fish oil have a strong foundation in physiological theory and *peer-reviewed scientific and clinical studies.*" (Emphasis added.)

It should be noted that the only literature you will find quoted in the bibliography of this book is from *"peer-reviewed scientific and clinical studies."* What this means to the reader is that the only references included here have been vigorously tested and researched at the research bench or in the clinical arena. Anecdotal information is not part of the scientific research used to substantiate the findings in this book.

Why was this information reviewed on the editorial page of *Hepatology*? Two studies published in that same volume demonstrated that omega-3 fatty acids can be protective of liver injury. Additionally, abnormal omega-6 to omega-3 fatty ratios correlates with enhanced liver injury and fatty liver formation that is seen in NAFLD. While these investigations involved animal models, the findings certainly seem applicable to humans given my findings and knowledge about intravenous feedings (see above). The same theme as seen in previous chapters is true for liver injury as well. Balanced omega-6 /omega-3 fatty acid ratios decreased the inflammatory response as measured by reduced liver chemistries and microscopic liver damage. These findings were associated with decreased expression of the pro-inflammatory substrates (see chapter 4). Again, this pro-inflammatory substrate expression is seen with excess omega-6/Trans fat ingestion and/or a deficiency of omega-3 fatty acid intake.

Type II diabetes is becoming rampant in America. One of the common themes seen in patients afflicted with this insulin-resistant form of diabetes is that nearly all suffer from fatty liver, and some go on to develop NAFLD. Numerous studies now reveal that Trans/omega-6 fats increase insulin resistance while **omega-3 fatty acids reduce insulin**

resistance. Insulin resistance leads to fat deposition in the liver which can lead to NAFLD. Studies have not yet been published looking at the efficacy of omega-3 fats in this group of patients with NAFLD, but it certainly seems intuitive that improved insulin resistance can only help reduce the fat-induced liver injury that I have seen in patients without diabetes who suffer from NAFLD.

Pearls

- **Omega-3 fatty acid supplementation reduces fatty liver**
- **Omega-3 fat deficiency causes damage to the liver**
- **The American diet is causing fatty liver disease**

"I have never let my schooling interfere with my education." Mark Twain

Chapter 11

Fat and the Inflamed Intestine

One of my patients who is afflicted with Crohn's disease went skiing one Sunday a few winters ago. He and his son skied through the morning and worked up a great appetite. They stopped for lunch at the ski lodge cafeteria, where the twosome devoured a large plate of French fries. This probably was not such an unusual meal, but that evening my patient found himself in a local hospital emergency room suffering from a flare of his Crohn's disease. His disease manifested itself with severe abdominal pain and intestinal bleeding. My patient's Crohn's disease had been in remission for the previous two years. He was on a treatment regimen that included prescribed medications, strict avoidance of "commercially" fried potatoes and a daily consumption of omega-3 oil.

The first question I asked him when I evaluated him was, "So, what did you eat?" He sheepishly said, "French fries." In this case, he ate a large plate of the tasty morsels. Additionally, he had been noncompliant with his daily omega-3 oil ingestion.

The reason I had given him strong counsel to avoid fried potatoes was that there is published evidence demonstrating that natural chemicals found in potatoes will bind to "manufactured" cooking oil in a way that will cause Crohn's disease to flare up, as happened so suddenly in my patient.

I have all of my patients suffering from Crohn's disease on omega-3 fats. This patient's story is a valuable lesson that has served him well as he has become more compliant with his diet, and he has not had another flare since his emergency room visit.

It is amazing how often I hear this type of medical history from patients who suffer from inflammatory bowel diseases. They pay a dear price for consuming the great American diet.

What is inflammatory bowel disease (IBD)? Inflammatory bowel disease is a generic name for a heterogeneous group of disorders that chronically and recurrently inflame the gastrointestinal system. The two most commonly recognized IBD disorders are Crohn's disease (as seen in my patient described above) and ulcerative colitis. The prevalence of these disorders is dramatically increasing in America, and they are affecting younger and younger age groups. While the specific cause or causes is unknown, it is clear that there are genetic, immunologic and environmental contributions to IBD. We cannot alter genetic risk factors at the present time. Most of the treatment has been directed toward reducing inflammation and most recently, manipulating the immune system. Not much attention has been directed toward environmental contributions, specifically, the great American diet.

I was intrigued when I read about a novel treatment trial published in *The New England Journal of Medicine* in 1996. A group of patients who suffered from Crohn's disease were randomized to either receive placebo or an enteric coated fish oil supplement. The results were nothing short of amazing.

The placebo group had a relapse rate of their Crohn's disease of 74% while the fish oil treated group had only a 41% relapse rate. While this treatment was far from perfect, it was almost twice as good as the placebo treatment, and it was one of the highest remission rates (59%) for treatments available for Crohn's disease at that time.

A second study was performed in Italy. A group of children with Crohn's disease were randomized to medication or medication plus omega-3 fatty acids. There was a higher remission rate in the omega-3 fat supplemented patients. This could be confirmed by measuring omega-3 fatty acid levels in the tissues of patients. There was a positive correlation of tissue levels of omega-3 fat and remission.

A short time later I learned about the inflammatory properties of fried potatoes (published in the *Crohn's and Colitis Journal*). It was now becoming clear to me why I was seeing a patient every week that suffered from a new diagnosis of IBD. They all participate in consuming potato chips, French fries, hash brown potatoes, and various other brand name fried fast food potato products. Couple this with a significant deficiency of omega-3 fatty acids in the diet of the youth of America, and we have a setup for IBD in the genetically susceptible individual. Because of these bits of information, I began counseling my patients about the importance of consuming omega-3 fats and the discontinuation of fried potato products. While I have not always been successful in keeping patients in remission, many of them are doing very well.

The biggest challenge I have been faced with is convincing patients about the essential nature of essential fatty acids, and specifically, the anti-inflammatory role that omega-3 fatty acids play in IBD. The American diet is rich in omega-6 fatty acids, and it is depleted of omega-3 fatty acids. Because of these facts, the omega-6 to omega-3 ratio in our diet is quite high. This imbalance contributes to excess production of pro-inflammatory substances (see Chapter 4). These dietary aberrations are environmental factors that can be modified by patients with IBD in an attempt to reduce disease activity. They can also be altered in the "natural" foods we consume such as eggs, milk, and meat. Animals fed diets rich in omega-6 fat will have a high content of omega-6 fat in their eggs, milk and meat. Alternatively, if animals are fed diets rich in omega-3 fat, their farm products are rich in this fat.

Over the last several decades, animals have been caged, fattened rapidly with diets rich in omega-6 fats and then passed on to the consumer. A recent study revealed that cattle fed a pastured diet had a high content of omega-3 fat in their meat, whereas cattle fed grain in a feedlot had meat high in omega-6 fat. If we consume a diet with farm products rich in omega-6 fat, that fat is incorporated into our bodies. Likewise, if we consume a diet of farm products rich in omega-3 fat, that fat is incorporated into our bodies. I have had numerous patients tell me over the past several years that one of the triggers that causes a flare in their bowel inflammation is consuming beef, pork or dairy products. No wonder. These foods are loaded with omega-6 fats because of modern farming practices as I have mentioned above.

In patients with Crohn's disease, data show that intestinal tissue is nearly totally depleted of omega-3 fats. Other studies show that milk rich in omega-6 fat exacerbate intestinal inflammation while omega-3 fat rich milk suppresses this inflammation in an animal model. It is important for all of us to understand that America has moved our cattle out of the pasture and into the feedlot since the 1930's. This has steadily increased the amount of omega-6 fat in the American diet. Hence, a steady increase in IBD has been seen as well.

I had been confused in the past about the lack of improvement of patients with inflammatory bowel disease (IBD) supplemented with omega-3 fats. It is clearer to me now.

None of these studies made any attempt to reduce the intake of omega-6/Trans fat in these patients. Perhaps future studies will help to define the appropriate ratio of omega-6: omega-3 fats as well as the appropriate amount and type of omega-3 fatty acids needed to help facilitate reduction of the inflammation seen in IBD. As can be seen in the patient I introduced you to in the beginning of this chapter, the role of fat ingestion along with medical therapy plays an important part in managing patients with IBD.

Pearls

- **"Commercially" fried potatoes cause inflammation in the intestine**
- **Omega-3 fatty acids reduce inflammation in the intestine**
- **A balance of omega-3 and omega-6 fat is essential in patients with inflammatory bowel disease**

"Honesty is the first chapter in the book of wisdom." Thomas Jefferson

Chapter 12

Lung Disease and Lipids

A sthma is a syndrome characterized by recurrent, reversible bouts of respiratory distress associated with wheezing, shortness of breath, and cough. It is a significant, chronic medical condition that now affects one in ten Americans. This disorder has become one of the major health problems facing people in the United States in just the past 35 years. Demographics reveal a steady increase in the prevalence of asthma over that same time period.

When I grew up in a small town in north Idaho in the late 1950's and 1960's, I graduated from a high school class of 213 students. Not one of us suffered from asthma. We all grew up without fast food restaurants. We ate farm products from animals that had not been raised on feedlots. We had been consuming cod liver oil as a state requirement to prevent rickets of the bones. We started the first decade of our lives drinking unpasteurized milk. Were any or all of these factors contributory to the fact that none of my generation suffered from asthma while we were growing up?

While the cause of asthma has never completely been discovered, it is now clear that there is continued inflammation in the airways of the lungs. This inflammation can be worsened by "allergic" stimuli such as grass, pollens, peanuts, and many other reported triggers. Excess arachidonic acid leads to the production of inflammatory substances, called leukotrienes. These leukotrienes worsen the breathing condition of the asthmatic patient. As you may recall from the chapter on fatty acids, omega-6 fatty acids are converted to arachidonic acid by the liver. The arachidonic acid then generates these pro-inflammatory leukotrienes.

In the 1960's to the present, the omega-6 fatty acid content dramatically increased in the American diet with the explosion of the fast food industry. Additionally, the omega-3 fatty acid content of our diet decreased with the discontinuation of cod liver oil in the daily diet, the nationwide pasteurization of milk, and the development of feedlot farming (feeding animals a diet rich in omega-6 fats rather than the omega-3 diets of grass-fed cattle). It is thought that this shift from omega-3 fats to omega-6 fats in our diet led to excess pro-inflammatory leukotrienes. In turn, we are witnessing the explosion of asthma in America.

Research exploring this thought has been quite revealing. A population-based epidemiologic study published in 1996 from Australia revealed a three-fold reduction in the prevalence of asthma in children who consumed fish more than once per week compared to those who ate no fish. Similar findings have now been reported in the American and European medical literature. Interestingly, this holds for adults as well. Why would this be so? Diets rich in fish are rich in omega-3 fats. Diets rich in omega-6 fats cause an increase in pro-inflammatory arachidonic acid metabolites (leukotrienes). Additionally, IgE levels are increased with an omega-6 rich diet. All of these substances are increased in patients suffering from asthma.

Several studies recently published document the improvement in asthmatic patients when they are placed on omega-3 fatty acid supplementation. The higher the omega-3 fat ingestion and the lower the omega-6: omega-3 fatty acid ratio, the more positive the modulator effect on asthma. In prospective, randomized studies of asthmatic patients we see:

- an improvement in exercise-induced asthma;
- a decrease in need for asthmatic medications;
- a significant improvement in lung function tests; and
- a decrease in allergic reactions.

Not all the data is as convincing though. A study in Australia randomized babies to a diet rich in omega-6 fats or omega-3 fats. The results demonstrated only a 10% reduction in the prevalence of wheezing in the omega-3 fatty acid-supplemented group compared to the group consuming the diet rich in omega-6 fats at 18 months of age. Even though the trend in response was in the right direction, it did not reach statistical significance (so much for statistics) for the scientific community. Asthma is typically diagnosed around five years of age, and this study is now following these patients out to that age to see if "statistical significance" will be reached.

A second study from the same time period, again from Australia, did find a statistically significant reduction of asthma in childhood that was associated with increased omega-3 versus omega-6 fat ingestion. Interestingly, this study was in 6- to 8-year-old children.

At the time of the writing of this book, The National Asthma Education and Prevention Program of The National Institutes of Health has made no reference to any of the information included in this chapter. Epidemiologic studies, analyses of specific biochemical markers of inflammation associated with asthma, and clinical outcome trials all suggest and support recommending a reduction of omega-6 fats and an increase of omega-3 fat in our diet. My own life experience and the data support this view. I am curious how long it will take for the National Institutes of Health to appreciate this data.

Pearls

- **Omega-3 fatty acids reduce asthma**
- **Excess omega-6 fats worsen asthma**

"Knowledge does not come to us in details, but in flashes of light from heaven." Henry David Thoreau

Chapter 13

Fattening Up Our Nerves
❦

Vision

When I was a kid in grade school none of us needed to wear glasses, despite the fact that the school nurse checked our vision twice per year. By the time I graduated from High School, nearly all of us needed glasses. Omega-3 fat had been dramatically decreased in the American diet beginning when I was eight years old (see Chapter 4) with the pasteurization of milk and the discontinuation of cod liver oil supplementation. Seven years later I needed glasses as did most of my classmates. Was this just a coincidence or was there a connection?

British physicians in the 1800's learned that children given cod liver oil would be spared night blindness. The mechanism of this preventative measure was unknown to the doctors. The 20th century brought a rapid expansion of the understanding of the mechanisms of disease states, protein, fat, vitamin and mineral deficiencies, and biochemical pathways involved in normal physiology. When cod liver oil supplementation was discontinued in the Western diet in the early 1960's, scientists did not realize the importance of omega-3 fats as they did the essential vitamins (especially vitamin A and D) found in abundance in this oil. When pasteurization of milk was initiated, it was fortified with vitamin A to prevent night blindness but was not fortified with omega-3 fat found in the fish oil. Consequently, children all over America began to require reading glasses by the millions. Today, the vast majority of the youth of the United States require visual correction.

Studies in the past ten years are now shedding light on the reason behind this. One of the fats found in abundance in omega-3 fat found in fish oil is called docosahexaenoic acid or DHA. This fatty acid is found in abundance in the brain and eye. During human development and growth, DHA intake is essential for normal vision development. Hence, decreased visual acuity is seen in our DHA-deficient youth.

Other **eye problems** are now associated with **omega-3 fat deficiency** and possibly may be prevented or partially corrected with dietary supplementation. These include:

- **Visual acuity**
- **Age-acquired macular degeneration**
- **Glaucoma**

Visual acuity may be developed properly in prenatal and childhood development with adequate omega-3 fat supplementation in the diet. It is less clear whether visual acuity can be improved in adulthood by similar supplements.

Both age-acquired macular degeneration and glaucoma can be prevented or visual loss from these two eye diseases reduced with omega-3 fat ingestion. Age-related macular degeneration is a disease of the retina found on the back of the eye. This disorder leads to blindness and is a major cause of disability in the geriatric population.

Glaucoma is a disease of the eye where there are abnormal fluid pressures and/or flows inside the eye. This can lead to visual loss over time, and eventually blindness without treatment.

Some investigations have provided equivocal results with omega-3 fat supplementation. These studies did not try to control Trans omega-6 fat ingestion or try to reduce the omega-6 to omega-3 fat ratios in the diet of the individuals being evaluated. Both of these factors may be important variables in fat metabolism as can be seen in many of the previous chapters. It will be curious to see the state of human vision in the next few decades as more and more mothers now beginning to realize the importance of omega-3 fat supplementation to the health of their children.

Depression

When I was in medical school in the late 1970's, I was taught that children rarely suffer from bipolar disorder (manic-depressive disorder); that this was a disorder affecting only adults. Depression also was considered a disorder that affected adults. Modern research reveals that:

- Approximately 20% of the 21 million individuals affected with these mood disorders are adolescent youths. That is a staggering **4 million young people**.
- The suicide rate of youths aged 5- to 24-years-old has tripled since 1960.
- Over 30,000 people kill themselves annually in the United States.
- Of the approximately 400,000 people who attempt suicide each year, 250,000 individuals need medical assistance for suicide attempts.

- More than three college students die from depression-induced suicide every day in America.
- Suicide rates increase with age.

Is there a connection with the rise in these mood disorders in the population and omega-3 fat deficiency in America?

As mentioned above, the human brain contains highly concentrated levels of omega-3 fats. The exact role of these fats in brain chemistry and function has not been clearly defined. Population-based, epidemiologic studies (a look back at the population without initiating a treatment such as omega-3 fat supplementation) have revealed a protective effect of omega-3 fats for depression disorders. Several prospective, randomized studies also demonstrate this protective effect of omega-3 fatty acid supplementation in individuals suffering from mood disorders. The mania aspect of bipolar disorder does not seem to benefit as much with essential fatty acid supplementation.

Every individual who suffers from depressive mood disorders certainly cannot blame it solely on omega-3 fat deficiency. It is clear, though, from the epidemiologic studies, the rise in mood disorders since the 1960's and the clinical improvement in many of those affected by depression with omega-3 fat supplementation that these oils play a significant role in the mental health of many people.

Dementia – The Omega of Fat Metabolism

When I was in medical school 30 years ago, I rarely saw patients affected with severe dementia. Today, never a single day goes by in my medical practice without seeing a patient who suffers from some form of dementia.

As a teenager, I remember a family plagued with breast cancer, dementia, and Parkinson's disease. We all attributed it to "bad genes." Clearly my thoughts have changed. It

saddens me to think that almost 20% of the American population will suffer from significant dementia before they die.
I recall attending large family reunions in my youth. No
one suffered from significant dementia. That is certainly not
the case today. Is the rise in the incidence and prevalence of
dementia solely due to the fact that people live longer today,
or are there any causal factors in play related to fat consumption in our diet?

Several population studies published in the past decade
show an association between a susceptibility to Alzheimer's
disease and high blood levels of cholesterol. Other research
studies also confirm the observation that adults in mid-life
with elevated serum cholesterol are at increased risk of developing dementia later in life. Interestingly, if you develop
elevated cholesterol in your senior years, that susceptibility is not seen. As discussed in the chapter concerning
the fundamentals of fats, the consumption of manufactured
Trans fats leads to the elevation of the "bad" LDL cholesterol and lowers the "good" HDL cholesterol. Omega-3 fatty
acids lower your LDL cholesterol. These observations and
associations do not prove a cause-effect process, however.

Does the evidence suggest a causal relationship between
omega-3 fat deficiency and dementia?

The normal brain contains very high levels of omega-
3 polyunsaturated fatty acids. While all of the brain functions have not been determined, it is quite clear that these
essential fats are intimately involved with the biochemistry,
physiology, and presumably the pathology of your brain.

It was appreciated as early as 1929 that brain function is
dependent on essential fats (see chapter 1). This was reaf-
firmed in the 1970's when it was determined that omega-3 fats
were the essential fats required for cognitive development.
During the past quarter century numerous studies involving
children and middle-aged adults supported this. Studies also
now reveal that omega-3 fats reduce progression of very

early dementia, although not for more advanced disease. I believe that once damage to the brain is too far advanced, not much can be done to reverse this process.

The two parts of the brain affected by Alzheimer's disease and Parkinson's disease (another disorder associated with the development of dementia) have been found to have omega-3 fat deficiency in those parts of their diseased brains. Another disease, schizophrenia, is associated with the inability to smell normally. The same part of the brain affected by schizophrenia (the olfactory cortex) is also associated with omega-3 fatty acid deficiency.

Data from animal studies and human population studies provide emerging evidence that atherosclerosis of the brain is contributory to the development of Alzheimer's disease and other forms of dementia. Disturbed cholesterol metabolism is rampant in America. Five percent of children and 45% of middle-aged adults suffer from this disordered metabolism. As I pointed out in Chapter 5, there is a very important class of polyunsaturated fats (conjugated linoleic acids) that prevents atherosclerosis formation. As America shifted from grassland-fed cattle in favor of stockyard fattened cattle, the conjugated linoleic acids found in the milk, dairy products, and meat declined as well. Not much data is available in the medical literature that addresses how much this is contributing to the rise of atherosclerosis-associated dementia in America.

My conjecture at this juncture is that:

- the **increase in manufactured Trans fat consumption** (with its negative effects of serum cholesterol);
- the **loss of omega-3 fat consumption** (with its direct protective effect on the brain); and
- the **loss of conjugated linoleic acid** (with its protective effect against atherosclerosis formation) all have

contributed to the **increase in dementia** seen in America in the past 50 years.

Pearls

- **Omega-3 fat deficiency is associated with eye diseases**
- **Depression is improved with omega-3 fat supplementation**
- **Dementia is associated with excess omega-6 fat ingestion, Trans fat-induced elevated cholesterol, and omega-3 fat deficiency**

"Live with enthusiasm! Years wrinkle the skin, but to give up enthusiasm wrinkles the soul." General Douglas MacArthur

Chapter 14

When Skin Meets Fat

One of the receptionists in my office suffered from psoriasis of the skin. Psoriasis is a scaling skin condition that can be quite annoying, to say the least, because the skin becomes itchy, red and flaky. Numerous treatments have been developed over the years in an attempt to control psoriasis. My receptionist had been treated with steroid creams, light treatments, and the like without much benefit.

Psoriasis is just one of many immune-mediated, incurable skin disorders. According to the National Institutes of Health, psoriasis alone affects almost **eight million Americans**.

One day I asked my receptionist what medication she was taking for her psoriasis. She told me that she had given up because nothing seemed to help. Because of my literature research concerning essential fatty acids, I asked her if she had tried taking flax seed oil. I had just found an article describing intravenous infusion of this omega-3 fatty acid for the treatment of patients with refractory psoriasis. The conclusion of this research study was that intravenous omega-3 oil infusion caused many patients to go into clinical remission of their psoriasis compared to placebo-treated subjects. I then reviewed several other infusion studies of omega-3 fat that all found similar effective results.

Now the treatment of psoriasis is outside the purview of my clinical practice. But as a doctor I knew that 6,000 mg of flax seed oil per day provided the upper dosing range for the recommended daily allowance of omega-3 fats. (It certainly wouldn't hurt her, and it might help.) Within days she noticed significant improvement in her itchy, scaly condition. By the end of a couple months her skin condition was under better control than she could ever remember. **Flax seed oil helps psoriasis!**

Several studies have been published looking at the benefits of fish oil supplementation with mixed results. As early as 1988 a paper appeared in *The Lancet* demonstrating clinical improvement in all measured skin parameters (itching, redness, scaling) in psoriasis patients given 10 capsules of fish oil per day for 8 weeks compared to placebo-treated subjects.

Other studies of orally administered omega-3 oil have not found much benefit. The reason for this most likely is a dose effect. The richest source of omega-3 fatty acids by far is flax seed oil. The dose of fish oil needed to be comparable to flax seed oil would be doses far exceeding most any fish oil treatment that has been studied. One of the concerns with high doses of fish oil supplementation is the potential excess ingestion of Vitamins A and D. Excess vitamin A can lead to significant liver damage if taken chronically. High levels of these vitamins are not found in flax seed oil.

The other skin condition that I would like to discuss is atopic dermatitis. This is a chronic, persistent, relapsing, inflammatory skin condition most commonly seen in children. Prior to 1960, approximately 2 to 5 % of children were affected with atopic dermatitis. The number of those with this skin problem has increased to as many as 20% of all children today. While there is clearly a genetic component to the expression of atopic dermatitis, the rise in the frequency of this skin disorder parallels the loss of omega-3 fat seen in America after 1960 (see Chapter 4). Several studies looking at several different omega-3 fatty acid supplements have been reported, including fish oil, borage oil, and evening primrose oil. The majority of the studies demonstrate a positive benefit without side effects in treating this annoying skin disorder. As stated earlier in the book, ingestion of omega-3 fats produces anti-inflammatory chemicals in the body while omega-6 fatty acids stimulate the production of pro-inflammatory chemicals involved with the pathophysiology of atopic dermatitis.

As the "fast food" industry dramatically led to increased consumption of omega-6 and Trans fat, the American diet had been made deficient in omega-3 fats. Pasteurization of raw milk, discontinuation of cod liver oil supplementation, and a shift to feedlot farming all contributed to this deficiency. These changes were a setup for inflammatory skin conditions to explode in the United States. With steps now mandated by the federal government to reduce Trans omega-6 fat ingestion in our diet, we may witness decreases in the prevalence of both psoriasis and atopic dermatitis in our youth.

Pearls

- **Omega-3 fat supplementation helps treat psoriasis**
- **Other skin disorders may benefit from elimination of Trans fat, reducing omega-6 fat, and omega-3 supplementation**

"Before I formed you in the womb I knew you,
before you were born I set you apart." Jeremiah 1:4

Chapter 15

Maternity: The Alpha of Fat Metabolism

Pregnancy

When my wife was pregnant, she was strongly encouraged not to consume alcohol, smoke cigarettes, or gain too much weight. It was also recommended that she exercise, drink plenty of water, take a prenatal vitamin, and eat healthy, well-balanced meals. Unfortunately, the Food and Drug Administration at the time had the "recommended food pyramid" upside down compared with the newly revised dietary recommendations that were released in 2005. It is only in the 2005 guidelines that omega-3 fats have now been included in the food pyramid.

It has been known since the 1920's that there are essential fatty acids required for normal brain function in the adult and brain development for the baby in the uterus as well as in the first developmental years of childhood. The 1970's revealed that this essential fat is omega-3 fatty acid.

Omega-3 fats are not stored in the human body to any degree other than in the brain. In fact, 90% of brain fat is omega-3. Because of this, the body requires continued, regular ingestion of omega-3 fatty acids to keep up with normal brain function. In the developing baby in the uterus, the mother's body supplies the baby with the omega-3 polyunsaturates needed for neurologic/brain growth and maturation.

If an expectant mother is already deficient in omega-3 fats in her own body, she becomes even more so during the pregnancy as she "feeds" her baby. The consequence of this is that both the newborn baby and the mother are deficient in this essential fat. The mother is then at increased risk of developing post-partum depression, emotional lability, and behavior disorders. **Studies have shown that post-partum depression is lowest worldwide where fish consumption is highest.** Additionally, controlled treatment trials cause improvement in mood disorders in post-partum mothers.

What's a mother to do?

It must be remembered that there are two essential fatty acids: omega-3 and omega-6 fatty acids. One without the other still leaves the mother and baby deficient. Both are required for normal childhood development and maintenance of health for the mother.

As can be seen from numerous discussions in previous chapters, we have an abundance of omega-6 fats in the Western diet. The mother needs to find nutritional sources of omega-3 fatty acids (see Chapter 6). Studies reveal that omega-3 fatty acid supplementations as well as diets rich in omega-3 fats are safe for both the mother and the baby. The mother will maintain her health, her mental health will be improved post-partum, and she will not be at increased risk of bleeding during childbirth (see next chapter).

The pregnancy story in relation to fat metabolism begins even before pregnancy. A recent study of women who suffer from ovulatory infertility were found to consume diets with higher levels of manufactured Trans fats and lower levels of essential fats. No data is available concerning the effects of omega-3 fat supplementation and infertility.

Some women are predisposed to developing gestational diabetes. **Women of short stature, increased body fat content, and consumers of diets rich in manufactured Trans fatty acids are at increased risk of developing diabetes during pregnancy.** What is worse, **these same women may pass on this problem to their babies**, all because of their diet. Like fetal alcohol syndrome, this is the "fetal fat syndrome"!

Two different animal models demonstrate that pregnant animals fed diets rich in manufactured Trans fatty acids cause their offspring to lose the insulin-regulating loss of appetite that lead to obesity of young adult animals. The animal brains actually had fewer insulin receptors that signal a decrease in appetite compared with the animals that had not been on diets rich in Trans fats. Whether this same mechanism is the cause of obesity in the youth of America today is not known as brain autopsy studies are not available for analysis. However, two different animal models reveal the same findings.

Maternal consumption of fish rich in omega-3 fats or supplements containing omega-3 fats has significant benefits for the baby. Data now show that:

- pre-term deliveries are less frequent,
- low gestational weight babies are less frequent,
- early childhood asthma is less frequent,
- atopic dermatitis/eczema occurs less frequently, and
- early mental processing skills are more advanced

if mothers have consumed their omega-3 fats during pregnancy. Additionally, if you recall from Chapter 4, the American diet is quite rich in omega-6 polyunsaturated fats.

The ratio of omega-6 fat to omega-3 fat is approximately 15:1 in favor of omega-6 fats.

Two recent studies using two different mammalian models (sheep and three different strains of mice) reveal that pregnant animals fed **diets rich in omega-6** fatty acid-supplemented diets **produce offspring that have:**

- **more aggressive behavior,**
- **decreased gestational size,**
- **decreased ability to feed,**
- **decreased locomotion ability, and**
- **decreased survival.**

Insights concerning the applicability of these animal studies to human development show data that is emerging concerning the treatment of **attention-deficit/hyperactivity disorder** (ADHD). Treatment of this disorder with essential fatty acids dates back 2500 years ago when Hippocrates treated children afflicted with a disorder, descriptively fitting ADHD, with a diet rich in essential fatty acids. Modern treatment trials suggest a benefit in placing children with ADHD on omega-3 fatty acid enrichment.

Not all children see the same benefit though. Perhaps this is due to irreversible effects of long-term exposure to manufactured Trans fats and/or the lack of reduction in the omega-6 to omega-3 fat ratio in the diet during the supplementation process. Much more research is needed in this area before the final word is in.

Suffice it to say, data point to a benefit of reducing manufactured Trans fat ingestion, increasing omega-3 fat ingestion, and decreasing omega-6 fat ingestion in relation to omega-3 fatty acid ingestion during pregnancy. This might seem complicated, but it is actually fairly easy:

(1) **Stay away from:**

- All pre-packaged foods (crackers, cookies, candies, cakes, etc.);
- "Fast foods" that are fried in oil (Fried potatoes, deep-fried meats, etc.); and
- All prepared foods containing Trans fats, "hydrogenated" or "partially hydrogenated fats."

(2) **Incorporate foods into your diet that are rich in omega-3 fatty acids** (see Chapter 4).

These changes will help your children become healthier, less prone to obesity, potentially smarter and less risk for the development of allergic disorders in their youth.

Breastfeeding

The last part of this chapter discusses breast feeding. Human breast milk is a highly nutritious, highly complex fluid that is now considered the best source for nourishment of infants. The content of the nutrients of breast milk varies during the first year after delivery. In the early weeks of lactation the milk contains high levels of fat. These fat levels decrease in the passing months. This high fat content is utilized by the infant to meet the needs of a rapidly growing nervous system, brain, vision, and mental development. Evidence is now overwhelming that children who have been breast fed have higher motor coordination skills and higher intelligence testing levels up to the age of four years old.

The fatty acids in the breast milk come either from the mother's diet or from her own body if she is not consuming them. Additionally, the fatty acid content in the milk varies depending on the diet of the mother. If her diet is rich in omega-6 fatty acids, more of these are passed on to the infant. Likewise, natural Trans fats and omega-6 fats vary in the breast milk depending on her intake of these fats. As we have learned earlier, the omega polyunsaturated fatty acids are essential to both the mother and the infant. If the mother is not ingesting enough for both her and child, the mother's body becomes depleted of these essential fats. This is probably contributory to the post-partum depression that can be seen that is reversible with omega-3 fatty acid supplementation. If both the mother and the infant are lacking in adequate omega-3 and omega-6 fat ingestion, the mother will be depressed, and the child will suffer neurologic and mental developmental delays. It is unclear whether the child will ever totally recover from these deficiencies.

In addition to the immediate mental and neurologic benefits of omega fats to the infant derived from the mother's breast milk, numerous other disorders later in life have a lower risk of developing in the breast-fed infant. Many of these diseases are inflammatory, autoimmune, or malignant in nature. It is not clear how many are dependent on the ingestion of omega fatty acids in the breast milk; but many are the same disorders that are dramatically reduced in adult life by the ingestion of omega-3 polyunsaturates. They include diseases such as:

- Asthma
- Breast Cancer
- Celiac Disease (allergy to gluten found in wheat, barley, rye)
- Crohn's Disease
- Diabetes
- Lymphoma
- Obesity
- Rheumatoid Arthritis

The omega-3 fatty acids found in fatty marine fish contain two polyunsaturated fatty acids: EPA (eicosapentaenoic acid) and DHA (docosahexaenoic acid). While both of the fatty acids are essential, DHA is the fatty acid that is most important in neurologic, mental, and visual development of the infant. The content of DHA in breast milk varies from 0.1% in mothers deficient in ingestion of fish oils to a high of 1.4% in mothers who consume marine fish regularly. **This is a 1,300% difference.** If women who do not consume omega-3 fatty acid rich fish are supplemented with fish oil, their breast milk content becomes enriched with DHA. The mother and the infant will benefit significantly.

The omega-3 fat found in plants is ALA (alpha linolenic acid). This fat is converted to DHA and EPA by the liver. If the mother is consuming significant quantities of omega-6 fatty acids or manufactured Trans omega-6 fatty acids, the conversion process of the ALA to DHA and EPA is slowed due to a common enzyme all of these fatty acids are competing for in the liver. If the mother is relying on plant-derived ALA (such as flax seed oil) as her source of omega-3 fatty acid, it is imperative that she avoid eating too much of these competitive fats, such as those found in Table 4 of Chapter 6.

Pearls

- **Maternal ingestion of omega-3 fats benefit babies from conception**
- **Maternal ingestion of omega-3 fats and subsequent breast feeding can help babies in their development**
- **ADHD may be reduced in children if expectant mothers avoid Trans fats**

"I am the Alpha and the Omega, the First and the Last, the Beginning and the End." Revelation 22:13

Chapter 16

No Side Effects to Omega-3 Fats

I was sitting at my desk working on some paperwork when one of my partners; I'll call him Dr. Bill, sat down next to me and asked if I had seen a report on the front page of *The Wall Street Journal* about the potential heavy metal toxicity that comes from eating fish regularly. I told him that I had not, and quizzed him about the article, later reading it with great consternation.

I had been telling my patients to eat more fish, fish oil, and flax seed oil for the past several years. Now, I immediately wondered if I was giving my patients poor advice. Worse, could I actually be placing their health at risk for more problems than they were already suffering from after three generations of omega-3 fatty acid deficiency and a century of the wrath of Trans omega-6 fat ingestion?

After reviewing numerous articles on the subject, I was relieved to find that the front-page article was misleading; in fact, it was completely wrong.

It is important to note at the outset of this chapter that, at the time of this writing, there are no reported life-threatening illnesses or deaths due to the consumption of omega-3 fatty acids. Scores of animal and human studies have documented absolutely no adverse complications following short and long-term ingestion of these fats. In 2004, the United States Department of Health and Human Services Agency for Healthcare Research and Quality published a review of over **20,000 subjects** reported in **148 research studies** and concluded that **there are no significant side effects associated with omega-3 fat ingestion**.

The most common complaints of consuming fish, fish oil, and other sources of omega-3 fatty acids are the aftertaste, burping and mild indigestion that bothers some individuals. I recall in my youth burping cod liver oil for hours after ingestion. My mom would give me a spoonful each morning and I would still be enjoying the taste until lunch. I am so appreciative of the new enteric coated fish oil capsules and I do not suffer the same eructation with them. Additionally, flax seed oil can cause indigestion and a change in bowel movements in a minority of people. The published studies containing a discussion of adverse gastrointestinal complaints report that 6.6% of people consuming omega-3 fats versus 4.3% of subjects consuming placebo substitutes noted these problems.

Four potential side effects of omega-3 fat ingestion are worthy of discussion. They include: heavy metal toxicity, increased risk of bleeding, increased risk of prostate cancer, and potential vitamin deficiency.

Heavy Metal Toxicity

The subject of heavy metal ingestion following consumption of fish and fish oil supplements was quite a concern to me. As I researched this intensely studied topic my anxiety soon evaporated. Mercury is one of five metals found throughout all of nature that occurs as a liquid at or near room temperature. It is not toxic to people in many insoluble forms. When it is found as an organic mercury compound, such as methyl mercury, it is toxic to the nervous system. This is the compound that is found in fish.

The United States Food and Drug Administration recommends that consumption of fish containing elevated levels of mercury (the most serious heavy metal of concern due to potential nerve damage) should be **limited to one serving** (7 ounces) **of fish per week**. High levels of mercury are levels greater than one part per million (approximately 1 microgram per gram of fish). For a seven-ounce piece of fish, that would represent 198 micrograms of mercury per week if it contained one part per million of mercury. Seven ounces of fish is 198 grams of meat. The federal government recommends that we not consume more than 198 micrograms (or 198 parts per million) of mercury in 198 grams (seven ounces) of fish per week.

Only four fish ever studied and published by the Food and Drug Administration have levels of mercury in this toxicity range: king mackerel, shark, swordfish, and tilefish.

None of these fish are on my menu. I did not even know what a tilefish was until I wrote this chapter! Tilefish, also called "golden bass" or "golden snapper," are found in the Pacific, Atlantic, and Indian oceans and are a reef fish. They range in size from small, colorful aquarium decorations to 50-pound edible "keepers." It is important for you to know that the **mercury warnings** about consumption of this fish are **from tilefish caught in the Gulf of Mexico**. The tilefish caught in this body of water have the highest mercury levels reported by the Food and Drug Administration at 1.450 parts per million (287 micrograms per seven ounces of fish). Remember, the most we are warned to consume is 198 micrograms per week.

The marine fish I prefer to consume (halibut, salmon, tuna, cod, etc.) contain far lower levels of mercury than tilefish found in the Gulf of Mexico. Albacore tuna has taken a "bad rap" in the press for its high levels of mercury compared to its "light tuna" counterpart. True, it has more mercury in it than light tuna. But, if you follow the Food and Drug Administration's guidelines for mercury exposure from fish ingestion, **you can safely eat 3-1/2 six-ounce cans of albacore tuna every week and still not exceed the upper limits of mercury exposure.**

Or 2 12-ounce jars of pickled herring per week.

Or, 71.4 ounces of salmon per week (that's 4-1/2 pounds or 10 servings of salmon per week).

I think your lips would start "puckering" like a fish with that much fish consumption.

Mercury levels have been measured in fish oil supplements as well. Many brands of commercial fish oil preparations (including the prescription omega-3 fat preparation called Omacor) do not even have detectable levels of this toxic metal. This is also true for vegetable sources of omega-3 fats such as flax seed oil. If you follow the Food and Drug Administration guidelines, you could drink 16-1/2 liters of oil per week of the brand of fish oil with the highest measured levels (12 micrograms per liter of oil). That is 4-1/3 **gallons** of fish oil per week.

One entire year's consumption of fish oil capsules is less than one quart per year!

The media hype surrounding mercury poisoning is misleading to the public. My nurses questioned me recently about mercury toxicity in fish oil capsules. They related to me their perception that fish oil capsules are unsafe due to potentially high levels of mercury. I quizzed them about the source of their information and found that their opinions were based solely on articles they had read in the newspaper and magazines.

One final note concerning the potentials of mercury toxicity. The most vulnerable times for significant toxic exposure for the child's brain are *in utero* during pregnancy and during early development years. A single study exists that suggests subtle neuropsychological changes in children born to mothers who consumed large amounts of whale meat (high in mercury) during their pregnancy. Again, how many women do you know who eat whale meat during pregnancy? Or at all for that matter? **No published data exists which demonstrates toxicity to children from regular fish ingestion.**

Increased Risk of Bleeding

Omega-3 fats found in fish oils are known to thin the blood. This is part of the reason why it is beneficial in preventing heart attacks. The blood does not clot in the blood vessel. This is a similar effect as is seen with small dose aspirin ingestion. At the time of this writing **no studies** have been published that demonstrate an increased risk of bleeding with fish oil or plant oil omega-3 fat supplementation. Additionally, patients who are also taking blood thinning agents such as aspirin or warfarin (coumadin) while consuming omega-3 supplements do not have increased risks of bleeding. Finally, bleeding during childbirth is no greater for women supplementing their diets versus those without fish oil intensification.

Increased risk of Prostate Cancer

The last area of concern relates to the reported relationship between prostate cancer and omega-3 fat ingestion. The confounding aspect of this literature is that various studies show an association, no association, and an inverse association with omega-3 fat supplementation and the occurrence of prostate cancer. When one sees a benefit and a detriment from the same studied substance (omega-3 fats) in humans, it tells me that there are other compounding issues that are not being controlled. In the writing of this book it has become clear to me that the major causes of cancer in this country are excess Trans fat in combination with omega-3 and conjugated linoleic acid ("natural" Trans fats) deficiency (see Chapter 8).

Potential Vitamin Deficiency

Another consideration with consuming omega-3 fatty acids is that we should also supplement our diet with a daily multivitamin.Taking a daily multivitamin ensures adequate intake of vitamins and minerals needed to take full advantage of incorporating these fatty fats into our cell membranes. It also helps the body manufacture many chemicals needed to reduce inflammation and regulate the immune response. These vitamins and minerals are essential co-factors in the utilization of all the essential fatty acids.

Finally, fresh omega-3 fatty acid supplements or fresh food sources of essential fatty acids should be purchased in small quantities, as they denature with heat and sunlight. Fatty acid supplements should be kept in the refrigerator to help ensure freshness. If your supplements taste rancid, they are rancid and should be discarded. Rancid oils can make you sick and are not good for the body any more than being deficient in fresh oils is good for the body.

Pearls

- **Omega-3 fats do not have any known toxicity**
- **Fish oil supplements do not contain dangerous levels of mercury**
- **One should take a multivitamin with omega-3 supplements**

"I will go after my lovers, that give me my bread and my water, my wool and my flax, mine oil and my drink." Hosea 2:5

Chapter 17

A Trip to the Grocery Store

I feel compelled to include this chapter because every time I go to the grocery store I am amazed at the challenges placed before me to try to comply with the good health standards outlined in this book.

For example, my wife and I were looking for a cake mix the other day. After we had examined every brand and flavor of cake mix in the entire baking section, the only cake mix that did not contain manufactured Trans fat (partially hydrogenated fat of one type or another) was an angel food cake mix. We settled on that. The next step was finding suitable frosting. There were no options available, so we resorted to making our own frosting (cherry chip vanilla) from scratch. It took a little longer than just scooping the pre-made frosting out of the plastic container, but the results were worth it.

The moral from this simple exercise was that I need to get out the cookbook and start baking real and fresh cakes again (like my mom used to do). Very little in a bakery gives you healthy options, as most everything there contains partially hydrogenated Trans fats. What is so misleading about all of this is that the bakery, the cake mix boxes or frosting mixes do not have to tell you the truth about the presence of manufactured Trans fats if a "single serving" contains less than 500 mgs of this dangerous fat. The Trans fat label will read "ZERO Trans fat," yet the fine print reveals just the opposite. It is amazing to me how small a "single serving" of cake appears to be (according to the manufacturers) when it comes to serving time. Obviously there is no room for "seconds."

As for other bakery goods, if enough of us stop in and talk to our bakers, we may have an impact at the local level to get them to start to rely on fresh, unadulterated bread products like our mothers and grandmothers made.

A great way to get away from the manufactured Trans omega-6 fats at the grocery store is to stay away from any processed foods. This is easier said than done for all of us, but the rewards will pay great dividends long term. While shopping for some crackers the other day, I was pleasantly surprised when I actually found a great-tasting multigrain and flax cracker that did not contain any manufactured Trans oils. It did have some unadulterated sunflower oil (rich in natural omega-6 oil) and canola oil (rich in omega-3 oil). It is all right to consume this combination, especially since the total fat content was quite low. Of note though, it was the only cracker in the entire store that did not contain processed Trans omega-6 fats. Yet all of the cracker packages on the shelves had claims that they did not contain Trans fats. If you can stick to the recommended "serving size" of "four crackers" the manufacturer comes in under the FDA radar for Trans fat labeling. But who can eat just four?

As I have mentioned earlier, it is easy to get omega-3 fats from fresh fish. The problem here is that fresh fish is rather expensive for most food budgets. One thing I have learned from cooking more fish in the past few years is that a typical serving for a person is about 3 to 4 ounces. You can have your butcher cut exactly the amount you need to minimize waste and cost.

The produce section is not as big of a challenge because the fats found in fresh fruits and vegetables are difficult to damage. Green, leafy vegetables are rich sources of omega-3 fatty acids as are many fruits. Not much can be done to negate the natural oils found in these products, except that fruits grown in the wild, or that are organically grown, have higher levels of these beneficial oils than commercially grown crops.

The meat and poultry industry is acutely aware of the education process underway in America concerning essential fatty acids. Because of this, we are starting to see beef in the fresh meat case that came from grass-fed rather than grain-fed sources. Chickens are being supplemented with omega-3 fat in their diets so that their eggs and meat will reflect the nutritional benefits to us at the dining room table. While you may have to pay a little more for these products now, the market demands for these far superior food products will eventually force the prices to come down. And, in the long run, the health benefits and decreased costs of chronic disease to your budget will be substantial. Getting to know your butcher, and your butcher knowing your desire for omega-3 rich meats, will help increase the demand for these products.

The dairy section is somewhat problematic in modern America. Pasteurization and homogenization has severely damaged the inherent beneficial fats of milk and its various products (cheese, cottage cheese, yogurt, cream, half and half, butter, ice cream, creamed cheese, etc.). A move is underway in many parts of the country to try to reverse the demands placed on the dairy industry by the federal government dating back to the 1950's and 60's. More dairies are starting to offer unpasteurized milk for sale. I would refer you to www.realmilk.com/where to find a dairy in your area that could supply you with unadulterated milk products. As demand for these vital products grows, more fresh milk outlets are sure to become available.

"We know that in all things God works for the good of those who love Him, who have been called according to His purpose." Romans 8:28

Chapter 18

So, How Do I Get Started?

As I bring this book to a conclusion, I find myself in a quandary. The average American is quite confused with the contents contained in this book; I know *I* was before I undertook the study and writing about this complex topic! Most of us have been convinced over the past 50 years that cholesterol and saturated fats are the cause of heart disease and cancer in the U.S. Now we are hearing that the combination of Trans fats and saturated fats are the cause of heart disease.

As I have tried to educate myself about the facts concerning fats I am reminded of the eloquent quotation by Mark Twain. He said, "I have never let my schooling interfere with my education." Wading through many of the thousands of articles and books published over the past 80 years has been a daunting task. But, it will have been worth it if you find my conclusions informative and applicable to your life.

I would like to recommend the following specific guidelines as a practicing gastroenterologist, teacher and life-long scientist:

- Try diligently to **eliminate all manufactured Trans omega-6 fats,** partially hydrogenated fats, or hydrogenated fats from your diet. They clearly are associated with many diseases of modern America. The federal government and the processed food industry are trying to placate the American public with unrealistic and deceptive labeling guidelines. **Read the fine print** describing the ingredients of all processed foods. If the label says that one of the ingredients is **hydrogenated or partially hydrogenated oil of any type, return the package to the shelf and find an alternative** (either from the grocery store shelf or from your cookbook). Talk to your local baker. See if he/she will eliminate these oils from their bakery items.

- **Do not be fearful of foods containing cholesterol or saturated fats**. These fats are not the culprits of the health nemesis we face in this country.

- Remember that there are **two essential fats: omega-3 and omega-6. Decrease your omega-6 fat intake while increasing your omega-3 fat intake**. If you can not do this through the grocery store on a daily basis, supplement your essential fatty acid intake with either a high quality fish oil or flax seed oil supplement. It is okay to mix these up a bit, but remember to take enough oil to get about **2,000 – 2,500 mg of omega-3** fatty acid **per day**. It is also better if you **divide your supplements into two-three servings per day**. Remember, that is how we eat our meals. Take a little bit of the oil with each meal. Fresh ground flax meal is also beneficial. You need about two tablespoons of ground flax for every two teaspoons of the oil.

- **Eat plenty of fresh, green leafy vegetables**. They are a great source of omega-3 fatty acids.
- **Eat omega-3 enriched meats and eggs**. You need to be an educated shopper. These products are available, but you have to look for them. Talk to your butcher. Have him or her acquire meats from grassland-fed animals rather than corn- or soybean-fed animals.
- **Include more fresh fish in your diet, especially fatty fish**. Fish is one of the best sources of omega-3 fats.
- **Try to include omega-3 rich foods in every meal** and in your snacks.

At the beginning of the second half of the 20th century America had returned from World War II, and Dwight D. Eisenhower was President of the United States. Most people today are unaware that this famous general and 34th President of our country suffered from Crohn's disease, premature heart disease and cerebrovascular disease. He suffered two heart attacks (1955, 1965) and a stroke (1957). He was afflicted with an intestinal inflammatory problem known as Crohn's disease much of his adult life. This malady led to surgeries to remove portions of his small intestine and colon.

What do all of these trivia of history have to do with this book? In retrospect, it is obvious to me that President Eisenhower suffered from a deficiency of an essential fat now known as omega-3 fatty acid or alpha linolenic acid. If General Eisenhower or his physicians had been aware of the contents of this book, he most likely would have had a much healthier life in his senior years.

While none of us has any guarantees in life, the sooner you initiate these guidelines into your diet, the sooner your body will benefit. One of the interesting things I have learned from researching this topic is that we have always had the desire to manufacture things that bring convenience, ease, or some other benefit to our lives. The amazing thing about the fruits, vegetables and animal products that are provided to us by our Maker is that they are perfect in their natural state. It is only when we started imposing our desire for improvement on these products that we bring havoc on our health. Perhaps if we return these food products to their "natural state" we can return to the health that our Maker wants us enjoy.

To your better health and a new life in **42 days**!

If you have any comments to pass on to me about the contents of this book, please send me an e-mail message to: info@42days.org.

Sincerely,

M. Frank Lyons II, M.D.

Bibliography

Adkinson: Middleton's Allergy: Principles and Practice, 6th Edition. Mosby, 2003. Asthma.

Al, M.D., van Houwelingen, A.C., Hornstra, G. Long-chain polyunsaturated fatty acids, pregnancy, and pregnancy outcome. American Journal of Clinical Nutrition 2000; 71 (Supplement): 285s-91s.

Albert, C.M., Campos, H., Stampfer, M., J., et al. Blood levels of long-chain n-3 fatty acids and the risk of sudden death. New England Journal of Medicine 2002; 346: 1113-8.

Albert, C.M., Hennekens, C.H., O'Donnell, C.J., et al. Fish consumption and risk of sudden cardiac death. Journal of the American Medical Association 1998; 279: 23-8.

Albuquerque, K.T. Intake of trans fatty acid-rich hydrogenated fat during pregnancy and lactation inhibits the hypophagic effect of central insulin in the adult of offspring. Nutrition 2006; 22: 820-9.

Alessandri, J.M., Guesnet, P., Vancassel, S., et al. Polyunsaturated fatty acids in the central nervous system:

evolution of concepts and nutritional implications throughout life. Reproduction, Nutrition, Development 2004; 44: 509-38.

Almendingen, K., Jordal, O., Kierulf, P. et al. Effects of partially hydrogenated fish oil, partially hydrogenated soybean oil, and butter on serum lipoproteins and Lp-A in men. Journal of Lipid Research 1995; 36: 1370-84.

Alpigiani, M.G., Ravera, G., Buzzanca, C., et al. The use of n-3 fatty acids in chronic juvenile arthritis. Pediatrica Medica E Chirurgica 1996; 18: 387-90.

Alwayn, I.P., Andersson, C., Zauscher, B., et al. Omega-3 fatty acids improve hepatic steatosis in a murine model: potential implications for the marginal steatotic liver donor. Transplantation 2005; 79: 606-8.

Arita, M., Bianchini, F., Aliberti, J, et al. Stereochemical assignment, anti-inflammatory properties, and receptor for the omega-3 lipid mediator resolving E1. Journal of Experimental Medicine 2005; 201: 713-22.

Ascherio, A.Epidemiologic studies on dietary fats and coronary heart disease. American Journal of Medicine 2002; 113: 9s-12s.

Ascherio, A., Katan, M.B., Zock, P.L., et al. Trans fatty acids and coronary heart disease. New England Journal of Medicine 1999; 340: 1994-8.

Ascherio, A., Rimm, E.B., Giovannucci E. L., et al. Dietary fat and risk of coronary heart disease in men: cohort follow-up study in the United States. British Medical Journal 1996; 313: 84-90.

Asherio, A., Rimm, E.B., Stampfer, M.J., et al. Dietary intake of marine n-3 fatty acids, fish intake, and the risk of coronary disease among men. New England Journal of Medicine 1995; 332: 977-82.

Astorg, P. Dietary fatty acids and colorectal and prostate cancers: epidemiological studies. Bulletin du Cancer 2005; 92: 670-84.

Ayton, A.K. Dietary polyunsaturated fatty acids and anorexia nervosa: is there a link? Nutritional Neuroscience 2004; 7: 1-12.

Babcock, T.A., Helton, W.S., Hong, D., Espat, N.J. Omega-3 fatty acid lipid emulsion reduces LPS-stimulated macrophage TNF-alpha production. Surgical Infections (Larchmont) 2002; 3: 145-9.

Babcock, T.A., Kurland, A., Helton, W.S., et al. Inhibition of activator protein-1 transcription factor activation by omega-3 fatty acid modulation of mitogen-activated protein kinase signaling kinases. Journal of Parenteral and Enteral Nutrition 2003; 27: 176-80.

Bagga, D., Wang, L., Farias-Eisner, R., et al. Differential effects of prostaglandin derived from omega-6 and omega-3 polyunsaturated fatty acids on COX-2 expression and IL-6 secretion. Proceedings of the National Academy of Science USA 2003; 100: 1751-6.

Barascu, A., Besson, P., LeFloch O., et al. CDK1-cyclin B1 mediates the inhibition of proliferation induced by omega-3 fatty acids in MDA-MB-213 breast cancer cells. International Journal of Biochemistry and Cell Biology 2006; 38: 196-208.

Barden, A.E., Mori, T.A., Dunstan, J.A., Taylor, A.L., et al. Fish oil supplementation in pregnancy lowers F2-isoprostanes in neonates at high risk of atopy. Free Radical Research 2004; 38: 233-9.

Baumgaertel, A. Attention-deficit/hyperactivity disorder: alternative and controversial treatments for attention-deficit/hyperactivity disorder. Pediatric clinics of North America 1999; 46: 977-92.

Bays, H.E. Safety considerations with omega-3 fatty acid therapy. The American Journal of Cardiology 2007; 99: 35c-43c.

Bazan, N.G. Omega-3 fatty acids, pro-inflammatory signaling and neuroprotection. Current Opinion in Clinical Nutrition and Metabolic Care 2007; 10: 136-41.

Beblo, S., Reinhardt, H., Muntau, A.C., et al. Fish oil supplementation improves visual evoked potentials in children with phenylketonuria. Neurology 2001; 57: 1488-91.

Belluzzi, A., Brignola, C., Campieri, M., et al. Effect of an enteric-coated fish-oil preparation on relapses in Crohn's disease. New England Journal of Medicine 1996; 334: 1557-60.

Belury, M.A. Inhibition of carcinogenesis by conjugated linoleic acid: potential mechanisms of action. Journal of Nutrition 2002; 132: 2995-8.

Bemelmans, W.J., Broer, J., Feskens, E.J., et al. Effect of an increased intake of alpha-linolenic acid and group nutritional education on cardiovascular risk factors: the Mediterranean alpha-linolenic enriched Groningen dietary intervention (MARGARIN) study. American Journal of Clinical Nutrition 2002; 75: 221-7.

Berbert, A.A., Kondo, C.R., Almendra, C.L., et al. Supplementation of fish oil and olive oil in patients with rheumatoid arthritis. Nutrition 2005; 21: 131-6.

Berth-Jones, J., Graham-Brown, R. Placebo controlled trial of essential fatty acid supplementation in atopic dermatitis. Lancet 1993; 341: 1557-60.

Bested, A.C., Saunders, P.R., Logan, A.C. Chronic fatigue syndrome: neurological findings may be related to blood-brain barrier permeability. Medical Hypotheses 2001; 57: 231-7.

Bjorkkjaer, T., Brunborg, L.A., Arslan, G., et al. Reduced joint pain after short-term duodenal administration of seal oil in patients with inflammatory bowel disease: comparison with soy oil. Scandinavian Journal of Gastroenterology 2004; 39: 1088-94.

Bogani, P., Galli, C., Villa, M., Visioli, F. Postprandial anti-inflammatory and antioxidant effects of extra virgin olive oil. Atherosclerosis 2007; 190: 181-6.

Bommareddy, A., Arasada, B.L., Mathees, D.P., Dwivedi, C. Chemopreventive effects of dietary flaxseed on colon tumor development. Nutrition and Cancer 2006; 54: 216-22.

Bourre, J.M. Where to find omega-3 fatty acids and how feeding animals with diet enriched in omega-3 fatty acids to increase nutritional value of derived products for human: what is actually useful? Journal of Nutrition, Health and Aging 2005; 9: 232-42.

Bourre, J.M. Dietary omega-3 fatty acids and psychiatry: mood, behavior, stress, depression, dementia and aging. Journal of Nutrition, Health and Aging. 2005; 9: 31-8.

Boure, J.M. Roles of unsaturated fatty acids (especially omega-3 fatty acids) in the brain at various ages during aging. The Journal of Nutrition, Health, and Aging 2004; 8: 163-74.

Bravi, F., Bosetti, C., Dal Maso, L., et al. Macronutrients, fatty acids, cholesterol, and risk of benign prostatic hyperplasia. Urology 2006; 67: 1205-11.

Brouwer, I.A., Katan, M.B., Zock, P.L. Dietary alpha-linolenic acid is associated with reduced risk of fatal coronary heart disease, but increased prostate cancer risk: a meta analysis. Journal of Nutrition 2004; 134: 919-22.

Brouwer, I.A., Zock, P.L., Wever, E.F., et al. A randomized controlled clinical trial on supplemental intake of n-3 fatty acids and the incidence of arrhythmia. European Journal of Clinical Nutrition. 2003; 57: 1323-30.

Broughton, K.S., Johnson, C.S., Pace, B.K., Liebman, M., Kleppinger, K.M. Reduced asthma symptoms with n-3 fatty acid ingestion are related to 5-series leukotriene production. American Journal of Clinical Nutrition 1997; 65: 1011-17.

Burdge, G. Alpha-linolenic acid metabolism in men and women: nutritional and biological implications. Current

Opinion in Clinical Nutrition and Metabolic Care 2004; 7: 137-44.

Burr, G.O., Burr, M.D. A new deficiency disease produced by the rigid exclusion of fat from the diet. Journal of Biological Chemistry 1929; 82: 364.

Burr, M.L., Fehily, A.M., Gilbert, J.F., et al. Effects of changes in fat, fish, and fiber intakes on death and myocardial reinfarction: diet and reinfarction trial (DART). Lancet 1989; 2: 757-61.

Calder, P.C. Dietary modification of inflammation with lipids. Proceedings of the Nutrition Society 2002; 61: 345-58.

Calder, P.C. N-3 polyunsaturated fatty acids and inflammation: from biology to the clinic. Lipids 2003; 38: 343-352.

Capanni, M., Calella, F., Centenaro, G. et al. Prolonged n-3 PUFA dietary supplementation improves fatty liver in patients with NAFLD. Aliment Pharmacol Therapy 2006; 23: 1143-51.

Calviello, G., Di Nicuolo, F., Gragnoli, S., et al. n-3 PUFA's reduce VEGF expression in human colon cancer cells modulation the COX-2/PGE2 induced ERK-1 and HIF-1alpha induction pathway. Carcinogenesis 2004; 25: 2302-10.

Chang, E.T. Nutrient intake and risk of non-Hodgkin's lymphoma. American Journal of Epidemiology 2006; 164: 1222-32.

Chavarro, J.E., Rich-Edwards, J.W., Rosner, B.A., Willett, W. C. Dietary fatty acid intakes and the risk of ovulatory infertility. American Journal of Clinical Nutrition 2007; 85: 231-7.

Chen, W., Jump, D.B., Grant, M.B., et al. Dyslipidemia, but not hyperglycemia, induces inflammatory adhesion molecules in human retinal vascular endothelial cells. Investigative ophthalmology and Visual Science 2003; 44(11): 5016-22.

Christensen, J.H., Korup, E., Asroe, J., et al. Fish consumption, n-3 fatty acids in cell membranes, and heart rate variability in survivors of myocardial infarction with left ventricular dysfunction. Am Journal of Cardiology 1997; 79: 1670-3.

Chua, B., Flood, V., Rochtchina, E., et al. Dietary fatty acids and the 5-year incidence of age-related maculopathy. Archives of Ophthalmology 2006; 124: 981-6.

Clark, K.L. Nutritional considerations in joint health. Clinics in Sports Medicine 2007; 26(1): 101-18.

Clarkson, T.W., Magos, L., Myers, G.J. The toxicology of mercury: current exposures and clinical manifestations. New England Journal of Medicine 2003; 349: 1731-7.

Coleman, H. Nutritional supplementation in age-related macular degeneration. Current Opinion in Ophthalmology 2007; 18(3): 220-23.

Covington, M.B. Omega-3 fatty acids. American Family Physician 2004; 70: 133-40.

Davidson, M. H. Mechanisms for the hypotriglyceridemic effect of marine omega-3 fatty acids. American Journal of Cardiology 2006; 98 (suppl): 27i-33i.

Dashti, N., Feng, Q., Franklin, F.A. Long-term effects of cis and trans monounsaturated (18:1) and saturated (16:1) fatty acids on the synthesis and secretion of apolipoprotein A-1 and apolipoprotein B-containing lipoproteins in HepG2 cells. Journal of Lipid Research 2000; 41: 1980-90.

Daviglus, M.L., Stamler, J., Orencia, A.J., et al. Fish consumption and risk of sudden cardiac death. New England Journal of Medicine 1997; 336: 1046-53.

De Caterina, R., Libby, P. Control of endothelial leukocyte adhesion molecules by fatty acids. Lipids 1996; 31: s57-s63.

DeFilippis, A.P., Sperling, L.S. Understanding omega-3's. American Heart Journal 2006; 151(3): 564-70.

De Groot, R.H., Hornsta, G., Van Houwelingen, A.C., Roumen, F. Effect of alpha-linolenic acid supplementation during pregnancy on maternal and neonatal polyunsaturated fatty acid status and pregnancy outcome. American Journal of Clinical Nutrition 2004; 79: 251-60.

De Lorgeril, M., Renaud, S., Mamelle, N., et al. Mediterranean alpha-linolenic acid-rich diet in secondary prevention of coronary heart disease. Lancet 1994; 343: 1454-9.

De Lorgeril, M., Salen, P., Martin, J.L., et al. Mediterranean diet, traditional risk factors, and the rate of cardiovascular complications after myocardial infarction final report of the Lyon Diet Heart Study. Circulation 1999; 99: 779-785.

De Luis, D.A. Dietary intake in patients with asthma: a case control study. 2005; 21(3): 320-4.

De Roos, N.M., Bots, M.L., Katan, M.B. Replacement of dietary saturated fatty acids by trans fatty acids lowers serum HDL cholesterol and impairs endothelial function in healthy men and women. Arteriosclerosis, thrombosis and Vascular Biology 2001; 21: 1233-7.

De Roos, N.M. Schouten, E.G., Katan, M.B. Consumption of a solid fat rich in lauric acid results in a more favorable serum profile in healthy men and women than consumption of a solid fat rich in trans-fatty acids. Journal of Nutrition 2001; 131: 242-5.

Dolecek, T.A. Epidemiological evidence of relationships between dietary polyunsaturated fatty acids and mortality in the multiple risk factor intervention trail: dietary PUFA and mortality. Proceedings of the Society of Experimental and Biological Medicine 2000; 177-82.

Duncan, A.M. The role of nutrition in the prevention of breast cancer. AACN Clinical Issues 2004; 15: 119-35.

Dwivedi, C., Natarajan, K., Matthees, D.P. Chemopreventive effects of dietary flaxseed oil on colon tumor development. Nutrition and Cancer 2005; 51: 52-8.

Dyerberg, J., Bang, H.O., Stoffersen, E., et al. Eicosapentaenoic acid and prevention of thrombosis and atherosclerosis? Lancet 1978; 2: 117-9.

El-Badry, A.M., Moritz, W., Contaldo, C., et al. Prevention of reperfusion injury and microcirculatory failure in macro-steatotic mouse liver by omega-3 fatty acids. Hepatology 2007; 45(4): 855-63.

Endres, S., Ghorbani, R., Kelley, V.E., et al. The effect of dietary supplementation with n-3 polyunsaturated fatty acids on the synthesis of interleukin-1 and tumor necrosis factor by mononuclear cells. New England Journal of Medicine 1989; 320: 265-71.

Enig, M.G. Know Your Fats: The complete primer for understanding the nutrition of fats, oils, and cholesterol. Bethesda Press, 2000.

Fan, Y.Y., Ly, L.H., Barhoumi, R., et al. Dietary docosa-hexaenoic acid suppresses T cell protein kinase C theta lipid raft recruitment and IL-2 production. Journal of Immunology 2004; 173: 6151-60.

Farrell, D.J. Enrichment of hen eggs with n-3 long-chain fatty acids and evaluation of enriched eggs in humans. American Journal of Clinical Nutrition 1998; 68: 538-44.

Ferrucci, L., Cherubini, A., Bandinelli, S., et al. relation-ship of plasma polyunsaturated fatty acids to circulating inflammatory markers. Journal of Clinical Endocrinology and Metabolism 2006; 91: 439-46.s

Fleith, M., Clandinin, M.T. Dietary PUFA for preterm and term infants: review of clinical studies. Critical Review of Food Science and Nutrition 2005; 45: 205-29.

Foran, S.E., Flood, J.G., Lewandrowski, K.B. Measurement of mercury levels in concentrated over-the-counter fish oil preparations: is fish oil healthier than fish? Archives of Pathology and Laboratory Medicine 2003; 127: 1603-1605.

Freeman, M.P., Hibbein, J.R., Wisner, K.L., et al. Omega-3 fatty acids: evidence basis for treatment and future research in psychiatry 2006; 67: 1954-67.

Freund-Levi, Y., Eriksdotter-Johnhagen, M., Cederholm, T., et al. Omega-3 fatty acid treatment in 174 patients with mild to moderate Alzheimer disease: OmegAD study: a randomized double-blind trial. Archives of Neurology 2006; 63: 1402-8.

Gadek, J.E., DeMichele, S.J., Karlstad, M.D., et al. Effect of enteral feeding with eicosapentaenoic acid, gamma-linolenic acid, and antioxidants in patients with acute respiratory distress syndrome: enteral nutrition in ARDS study group. Critical Care Medicine 1999; 27: 1409-20.

Gatto, L.M., Sullivan, D.R., Samman, S. Postprandial effects of dietary trans fatty acids on apolipoprotein (a) and cholesteryl ester transfer. American Journal of Clinical Nutrition 2003; 77: 1119-24.

GISSI-Prevenzione Investigators. Dietary supplementation with n-3 polyunsaturated fatty acids and vitamin E after myocardial infarction results of the GISSI-Prevenzione trial. Lancet 1999; 354: 447-455.

Goldberg, R.J., Katz, J. A meta analysis of the analgesic effects of omega-3 polyunsaturated fatty acid supplementation for inflammatory joint pain. Pain 2007; 129: 210-23.

Goldman: Cecil textbook of Medicine, 22nd edition: Asthma by J.M. Drazen. Saunders, 2004.

Goodstine, S.L., Zheng, T., Holford, T.R., et al. Dietary n-3/n-6 fatty acid ratio: possible relationship to premenopausal but not postmenopausal breast cancer risk in U.S. women. Journal of Nutrition 2003; 133: 1409-14.

Griel, A.E., Kris-Etherton, P.M., Hilpert, K.F., et al. An increase in dietary n-3 fatty acids decreases a marker of bone resorption in humans. Nutrition Journal 2007; 6: 2.

Grimble, R.F. Nutritional modulation of cytokine biology. Nutrition 1998; 14: 634-60.

Guermouche, B., Yessoufou, A., Soulimane, N., et al. n-3 fatty acids modulate T-cell calcium signaling in obese macrosomic rats. Obesity Research 2004; 12: 1163-70.

Hallaq, H., Smith, T.W., Leaf, A. Modulation of dihydropyridine-sensitive calcium channels in heart cells by fish oil fatty acids. Proceedings of the National Academy of Sciences USA 1992; 89: 17604.

Hardman, W.E. n-3 fatty acids and cancer therapy. Journal of Nutrition 2004; 134 (Supplement): 3427s-30s.

Harper, C.R., Jacobson, T.A. The fats of life: the role of omega-3 fatty acids in the prevention of coronary heart disease. Archives of Internal Medicine 2001; 161: 2185-92.

Harper, C.R., Jacobson, T.A. Usefulness of omega-3 fatty acids and the prevention of coronary heart disease. American Journal of Cardiology 2005; 96(11): 1521-9.

Harris: Kelley's Textbook of Rheumatology, 7th edition; Ch 90 – Metabolic Bone Disease by Nancy Lane and Meryl S. Leboff. Saunders; 2005.

Harris, W.S. Expert opinion: omega-3 fatty acids and bleeding – cause for concern? American Journal of Cardiology 2007; 99: 44c-46c.

Harris, W.S. n-3 fatty acids and serum lipoproteins human studies. American Journal of Clinical Nutrition 1997; 65: 1645s-54s.

Harris, W.S., Reid, K.J., Sands, S.A., Spertus, J.A. Blood omega-3 and trans fatty acids in middle-aged acute coronary syndrome patients. American Journal of Cardiology 2007; 99: 154-8.

He, K., Song, Y., Daviglus, M.L., Liu, K. et al. Accumulated evidence on fish consumption and coronary heart disease mortality: a meta analysis of cohort studies. Circulation 2004; 109: 2705-11.

Helland, I.B., Smith, L., Saarem, K., et al. Maternal supplementation with very long-chain n-3 fatty acids during pregnancy and lactation augments children's IQ at 4 years of age. Pediatrics 2003; 111: e39-44.

Heller, A.R., Rossier, S., Litz, R.J., et al. Omega-3 fatty acids improve the diagnosis-related outcome. Critical Care Medicine 2006; 34; 972-9.

Hodge, L., Salome, C.M., Hughes, J.M., et al. Effect of dietary intake of omega-3 and omega-6 fatty acids on severity of asthma in children. European Respiratory Journal 1998; 11: 361-65.

Hodge, W.G. Efficacy of omega-3 fatty acids in preventing age-related macular degeneration: a systematic review. Ophthalmology 2006; 113(7): 1165-72.

Holness, M. J., Smith, N. D., Greenwood, G.K., Sugden, M.C. Acute omeg-3 fatty acid enrichment selectively reverses high-saturated fat feeding-induced insulin hypersecretion but does not improve peripheral insulin resistance. Diabetes 2004; 53(suppl): s166-s71.

Horrobin, D.F. Essential fatty acid metabolism and its modification in atopic eczema. American Journal of Clinical Nutrition 2000; 201: 191-5.

Horrocks, L.A., Yeo, Y.K. Health benefits of docosahexaenoic acid (DHA). Pharmacology Research 1999; 40: 211-25.

Hu, F.B., Bronner, L., Willett, W.C., et al. Fish and omega-3 fatty acid intake and risk of coronary heart disease in women. Journal of the American Medical Association. 2002; 287: 1815-21.

Hu, F.B., Manson, J.E., Willet, W.C. Types of dietary fat and risk of coronary heart disease. Journal of the American College of Nutrition. 2001; 20: 5-19.

Hu, F.B., Stampfer, M.J., Manson, J.E., et al Dietary intake of alpha-linolenic acid and risk of fatal ischemic heart disease among women. American Journal of Clinical Nutrition 1999; 69: 890-7.

Hu, F.B., Stampfer, M.J., Manson, J.E., et al. Dietary fat intake and the risk of coronary heart disease in women. New England Journal of Medicine 1997; 337: 1491-9.

Hudert, C.A., Weylandt, K.H., Lu,Y., et al. Transgenic mice rich in endogenous omega-3 fatty acids are protected from colitis. Proceedings of the National Academy of Science USA 2006; 103: 11276-81.

Ibrahim, A., Natrajan, S., Ghafoorunissa, R. Dietary trans-fatty acids alter adipocyte plasma membrane fatty acid composition and insulin sensitivity in rats. Metabolism 2005; 54: 240-6.

Innis, S.M. Perinatal biochemistry and physiology of long-chain polyunsaturated fatty acids. Journal of Pediatics 2003; 143 (Supplement): s1-s8.

Innis, S.M. Dietary (n-3) fatty acids and brain development. Journal of Nutrition 2007; 137: 855-9.

Innis, S.M., Gilley, J., Werker, J. Are human milk long-chain polyunsaturated fatty acids related to visual and neural development in breast-fed term infants? Journal of Pediatrics 2001; 139: 532-8.

Innis, S.M., Pinsk, V., Jacobson, K. Dietary lipids and intestinal inflammatory disease. Journal of Pediatrics 2006; 149(Supplement): s89-s96.

Irons, R., Fritsche, K.L. Omega-3 polyunsaturated fatty acids impair in vivo interferon-gamma responsiveness ivia diminished receptor signaling. Journal of Infectious Diseases 2005; 191: 481-6.

Issa, A.M., Mojica, W.A., Morton, S.C., et al. The efficacy of omega-3 fatty acids on cognitive function in aging and dementia: a systematic review. Dementia and Geriatric Cognitive Disorders 2006; 21: 88-96.

James, M.J., Cleland, L.G. Dietary n-3 fatty acids and therapy for rheumatoid arthritis 1997; 27:85-97.

Jacobson, T.A. Secondary prevention of coronary artery disease with omega-3 fatty acids. The American Journal of Cardiology 2006; 98: 61i-70i.

Jayasooriya, A.P., Ackland, M.L., Mathai, M.L., et al. Perinatal omega-3 polyunsaturated fatty acid supply modifies brain zinc homeostasis during adulthood. Proceedings of the National Academy of Sciences USA 2005; 102: 7133-8.

Johnson, E.J., Schaefer, E.J. Potential role of dietary n-3 fatty acids in the prevention of dementia and macular degeneration. American Journal of Clinical Nutrition 2006; 83: 1494S-98S.

Jourdan, M.L., Matao, K., Barascu, C., et al. Increased BRCA1 protein in mammary tumours in rats fed marine omega-3 fatty acids. Oncology Reports 2007; 17: 713-9.

Judd, J., Clevidence, B., Muesing, R., et al. Dietary trans fatty acids: effects on plasma lipids and lipoproteins of healthy women and men. American Journal of Clinical Nutrition. 1994; 59: 861-8.

Jump, D.B. Fatty acid regulation of gene transcription. Critical Reviews in Clinical Laboratroy Sciences 2004; 41(1): 41-78.

Jump, D.B. Dietary polyunsaturated fatty acids and regulation of gene transcription. Current Opinion in Lipidology 2002; 13(2): 155-64.

Jump, D.B. The biochemistry of n-3 polyunsaturated fatty acids. Journal of Biological Chemistry 2002; 277: 8755-8.

Kalmijn, S., van Boxtel, M.P., Ocke, M., et al. Dietary intake of fatty acids and fish in relation to cognitive performance at middle age. Neurology 2004; 62: 275-80.

Kang, J.X. The importance of omega-6/omega-3 fatty acid acid ratio in cell function. The gene transfer of omega-3 fatty acid desaturase. World Review of Nutrition and Dietetics 2003; 92: 23-36.

Kelly, D.S. Modulation of human and inflammatory responses by dietary fatty acids. Nutrition 2001; 17: 669-73.

Kerscher, M., Korting, H. Treatment of atopic eczema with evening primrose oil: rationale and clinical results. Clinics in Investigative Medicine 1992; 70: 167-71.

Kompauer, I. Association of fatty acids in serum phospholipids with hay fever, specific and total immunoglobulin E. British Journal of Nutrition 2005; 93(4): 529-35.

Kris-Etherton, P.M., Harris, W.S., Appel, L.J. Omega-3 fatty acids and cardiovascular disease: new recommendations from the American Heart Association. Arteriosclerosis, Thrombosis and Vascular Biology 2003; 23: 151-2.

Kris-Etherton, P.M., Harris, W.S., Appel, L.J., et al. Nutrition C. Fish consumption, fish oil, omega-3 fatty acids, and cardiovascular disease. Circulation 2002; 106: 2747-57.

Kris-Etherton, P.M. Taylor, D.S., Yu-Poth, P., et al. Polyunsaturated fatty acids in the food chain in the United States. American Journal of Clinical Nutrition 2000; 71: 179-88.

Kromhout, D., Bosschieter, E.B., De Lezenne Coulander, C. The inverse relation between fish consumption and 20-year mortality from coronary heart disease. New England Journal of Medicine 1985; 312: 1205-9.

Kruger, M.C., Coetzer, H., deWinter, R., et al. Calcium, gamma-linolenic acid and eicosapentaenoic acid supplementation in senile osteoporosis. Aging 1998; 10: 385-94.

Kruger, M.C., Horrobin, D.F. Calcium metabolism, osteoporosis and essential fatty acids: a review. Progress in Lipid Research 1997; 36: 131-51.

Kumar: Robbins and Cotran: Pathologic basis of disease, 7th edition. Saunders, 2005. Chapter 2: Acute and chronic inflammation.

Kuroki, F. Serum n-3 polyunsaturated fatty acids are depleted in Crohn's disease. Digestive Diseases and Sciences 1997; 42(6): 1137-41.

La Guardia, M. Omega 3 fatty acids: biologic activity and effects on human health. Panminerva Med 2005; 47(4): 245-57.

Larsen: Williams Textbook of Endocrinology, 10th Edition; Osteoporosis. Saunders; 2003.

Leaf, A., Kang, J.X., Xiao, Y.F., Billman, G.E. N-3 fatty acids in the prevention of cardiac arrhythmias. Lipids 1999; 34: s187-s189.

Lee, K.N., Kritchevsky, D., Pariza, M.W. Conjugated linoleic acid and atherosclerosis. Atherosclerosis 1994; 108: 19-25.

Lee, J.Y. Plakidas, A., Lee, W.H., et al. Differential modulation of Toll-like receptors by fatty acids: preferential inhibition by n-3 polyunsaturated fatty acids. Journal of Lipid Research 2003; 44: 479-86.

Lee, S., Gura, K.M., Puder, M. Omega-3 fatty acids and liver disease. Hepatology 2007; 45: 841-5.

Leitzmann, M.F., Stampfer, M.J., Michaud, D.S. et al. Dietary intake of n-3 and n-6 fatty acids and the risk of prostate cancer. American Journal of Clinical Nutrition 2004; 80: 204-16.

Leung, I. Y. Nutritional manipulation of primate retinas, II: effects of age, n-3 fatty acids, lutein, and zeaxanthin on retinal pigment epithelium. Invest Ophthalmol Vis Science 2004; 45(9): 3244-56.

Lichtenstein, A.H., Ausman, L.M., Jalbert, S.M. et al. Effects of different forms of dietary hydrogenated fats on serum lipoprotein cholesterol levels. New England Journal of Medicine 1999; 340: 1933-40.

Lim, W.S., Gammack, J.K., Van Niekerk, J., Dagour, A.D. Omega-3 fatty acid for the prevention of dementia. Cochrane Database of Systematic Reviews 2006; 1; CD005379.

Lo, C.J., Chiu, K.C., Fu, M., et al. Fish oil decreases macrophage tumor necrosis factor gene transcription by altering the NF kappa-B activity. Journal of Surgical Research 1999; 82:216-21.

Loosemore, E.D., Judge, M.P., Lammi-Keefe, C.J. Dietary intake of essential and long-chain polyunsaturated fatty acids in pregnancy. Lipids 2004; 39: 421-4.

Lopez-Garcia, E., Schulze, M., Manson, J.E., et al. Consumption of (n-3) fatty acids is related to plasma biomarkers of inflammation and endothelial activation in women. Journal of Nutrition 2004; 134: 1806-11.

Lopez-Garcia, E., Schulze, M.B., Meigs, J.B., et al. Consumption of trans fatty acids is related to plasma biomarkers of inflammation and endothelial dysfunction. Journal of Nutrition 2005; 135: 562-6.

Lyons, J.J., Lyons, M.F., Meckler, K.A. A novel therapy for non-alcoholic steatohepatitis: essential fatty acids and ursodiol. American Journal of Gastroenterology 2007; 101:s160.

MacDonald, H.B. Conjugated linoleic acid and disease prevention: a review of current knowledge. Journal of the American College of Nutrition 2000; 19: 111s-18s.

Maclean, C.H., Issa, A.M., Newberry, S.J., et al. Effects of omega-3 fatty acids on cognitive function with aging, dementia, and neurological diseases. Evidence Report/ Technology Assessment (Summary) 2005; 114: 1-3.

Mann, G. Metabolic consequences of dietary trans fatty acids. Lancet 1984; 343: 1268;-71.

Marcason, W. How many grams of Trans-fat are recommended per day? Journal of the American Dietetic Association 2006; 106: 1507.

Martinez, M., Vasquez, E. MRI evidence of docosahexaenoic acid ethyl ester improve myelination in generalized peroxisomal disorders. Neurology 1998; 51: 26-32.

Massey, P. B. Dietary Supplements. Medical Clinics of North America 2002; 86(1): 127-47.

Mason: Murray and Nadel's Textbook of Respiratory Medicine, 4th Edition. Saunders, 2005. Chapter 37 – Asthma.

Masso-Welch, P.A., Zangani, D., Ip, C., et al. Inhibition of angiogenesis by the cancer chemopreventive agent conjugated linoleic acid. Cancer Research 2002; 62: 4383-9.

Matsuyama, W., Mitsuyama, H., Watanabe, M., et al. Effects of omega-3 polyunsaturated fatty acids on inflammatory markers in COPD. Chest 2005; 128(6): 3817-27.

Mathan, N.R., Welty, F.K., Barret, H.R., et al. Dietary hydrogenated fat increases high-density lipoprotein apoA-1 catabolism and decreases low-density lipoprotein apo-

B-100 catabolism in hypercholesterolemic women. Arteriosclerosis, Thrombosis and Vascular Biology 2004; 24: 1092-7.

Mattson, F.H., Hollenbach, E.J., Klingman, A.M. Effect of hydrogenated fat on the plasma cholesterol and triglycerides of man. American Journal of Clinical Nutrition 1975; 28: 726-31.

Mayer, K., Meyer, S., Reinholzl-Muhly, M., et al. Short-term infusion of fish oil-based lipid emulsions, approved for parenteral nutrition, reduces monocyted proinflammatory cytokine generation and adhesive interaction with endothelium in humans. Journal of Immunology 2003; 171: 4837-43.

Menendez, J.A., Ropero, S., Mehmi, I., et al. Overexpression and hyperactivity of breast cancer-associated fatty acid synthase (oncogenic antigen-519) is insensitive to normal arachidonic fatty acid-induced suppression in lipogenic tissues but it is selectively inhibited by tumoricidal alpha-linolenic and gamma-linolenic fatty acids: a novel mechanism by which dietary fat can alter mammary tumorigenesis. International Journal of Oncology 2004; 24: 1369-83.

Menendez, J.A., Vasques-Martaen, A., Ropero, S., et al. HER2 (erb2)-targeted effects of the omega-3 polyunsaturated fatty acid, alpha-linolenic acid (ALA; 18:3n-3), in breast cancer cells: the "fat features" of the "Mediterranean diet" as an anti-HER2 cocktail. Clinical and Translational Oncology 2006; 8:821-20.

Mensink, R.P. Metabolic and health effects of isomeric fatty acids. Current Opinions in Lipidology 2005; 16: 27-30.

Mensink, R.P., Katan, M. Effect of dietary trans fatty acids on high density and low-density lipoprotein cholesterol levels in healthy subjects. New England Journal Of Medicine 1990; 323: 439-45.

Mensink, R.P., Zock, P.L., Kester, A.D.M., Katan, M.B. Effects of dietary fatty acids and carbohydrates on the ratio of serum total to HDL cholesterol and on serum lipids and apolipoproteins: a meta analysis. American Journal of Clinical Nutrition 2003; 77: 1146-55.

Merchant, A.T. Intake of n-6 and n-3 fatty acids and fish and risk of community-acquired pneumonia in US men. American Journal of Clinical Nutrition 2005; 82(3): 668-74.

Mermer, C., Mercola, J. Omega-3's and childhood asthma. Thorax 2002; 57: 281.

Meydani, S.N. Modulation of cytokine production by dietary polyunsaturated fatty acids. Proceedings of the Society of Experimental and Biological Medicine 1992; 200: 189-93.

Mickleborough, T.D. Omega-3 fatty acids and airway hyper-responsiveness in asthma. Journal of Alternative and Complementary Medicine 2004; 10(6): 1067-75.

Mihrshahi, S., Peat, J.K., Marks, G.B., et al. Eighteen-month outcomes of house dust mite avoidance and dietary fatty acid modification in the childhood asthma prevention study. Journal of Allergy and Clinical Immunology 2003; 111: 162-68.

Mihrshahi, S., Peat, J.K., Webb, K, et al. Effect of omega-3 fatty acid concentrations in plasma on symptoms of asthma at 18 months of age. Pediatric Allergy and Immunology 2004; 15(6): 517-22.

Mischoulon, D. Update and critique of natural remedies as antidepressant treatments. Psychiatric Clinics of North America 2007; 30(1): 51-68.

Mischoulon, D., Maurizio, F. Depression: recent developments and innovative treatments. Docosahexanoic acid and omega-3 fatty acids in depression. Psychiatric Clinics of North America 2000; 23: 785-94.

Mishra, A., Chaudhary, A., Sethi, A. Oxidized omega-3 fatty acids inhibit NF-kappaB activation via a PPAR alpha-dependent pathway. Arterioscler Thromb Vasc Biology 2004; 24: 1621-27.

Mitchell, E.A. Clinical characteristics and serum essential fatty acid levels in hyperactive children. Clinical Pediatrics 1987; 15: 75-90.

Montuschi, P., Khartonov, S.A., Ciabattoni, G., et al. Exhaled leukotrienes and prostaglandins in COPD. Thorax 2003; 58: 585-8.

Morse, P., Horrobin, D., Manku, M., et al. Meta-analysis of placebo-controlled studies if the efficacy of Epogam in the treatment of atopic eczema: relationship between plasma essential fatty acid changes and clinical response. British Journal of Dermatology 1989; 121: 75-90.

Mosley, E.E., Wright, W.L., McGuire, M.K., McGuire, M.A. Trans fatty acids in milk produced by women in the United States. American Journal of Clinical Nutrition 2005; 82: 1292-7.

Mozaffarian, D.M., Ascherio, A., Hu, F.B., et al. Interplay between different polyunsaturated fatty acids and risk of coronary heart disease in men. Circulation 2005; 111: 166-73.

Mozafferian, D., Geelen, A., Brouwer, I.A., et al. Effect of fish oil on heart rate in humans: A meta analysis of randomized controlled trials. Circulation 2005; 112: 1945-52.

Mozaffarian, D., Katan, M.B., Ascherio, A., et al. Trans fatty acids and cardiovascular disease. New England Journal of Medicine 2006; 354: 1601-13.

Mozaffarian, D., Pischon, T., Hankinson, S.E., et al. Dietary intake of trans fatty acids and systemic inflammation in women. American Society for Clinical Nutrition 2004; 79: 606-12.

Mayser, P., Mrowietz, U., Arenberger, P., et al. Omega-3 fatty acid-based lipid infusion in patients with chronic plaque psoriasis: results of a double-blind, random-ized, placebo-controlled, multicenter trial. Journal of the American Academy of Dermatology 1998; 38: 539-47.

Nagakura, T., Matsuda, S., Shichijyo, K., et al. Dietary supplementation with fish oil rich in n-3 polyunsaturated fatty acids in children with bronchial asthma. European Respiratory Journal 2000; 16: 861-65.

Natvig, H., Borchgrevink, C.F., Dedichen, j., et al. A controlled trial of the effect of linolenic acid on incidence of coronary heart disease: the Norwegian vegetable oil experiment of 1965-66. Scandinavian Journal of Clinical Investigation Supplement 1968; 105: 1-20.

Ness, A.R., Hughes, J., Elwood, P.C., et al. The long-term effect of dietary advice in men with coronary disease: follow-up of the diet and reinfarction trial (DART). European Journal of Clinical Nutrition 2002; 56: 512-518.

Nestel, P.J., Pomeroy, S.E., Sasahara, T., et al. Arterial compliance in obese subjects is improved with dietary plant n-3 fatty acid from flaxseed oil despite increased LDL oxidizability. Arteriosclerosis, Thrombosis, and Vascular Biology 1997; 17: 1163-70.

Nestel, P., Shige, H., Pomerory, S., et al. The n-3 fatty acids eicosapentaenoic acid and docosahexaenoic acid increase systemic arterial compliance in humans. American Journal of Clinical Nutrition 2002; 76: 326-30.

Neuringer, M., Jeffrey, B.G. Visual development: neural basis and new assessment methods. Journal of Pediatrics 2003; 143: S87-S95.

Nguyen, C.T., Bui, B.V. Sinclair, A.J., Vingrys, A.J. Dietary omega-3 fatty acids decrease intraocular pressure with age by increasing aqueous outflow. Investigative Ophthalmology and Visual Science 2007; 48: 756-62.

Nielsen, A.A., Jorgensen, L.G., Nielsen, J.N., et al. Omega-3 fatty acids inhibit an increase of proinflammatory cytokines in patients with active Crohn's disease compared with omega-6 fatty acids. Alimentary Pharmacology and Therapeutics 2005; 22: 1121-8.

Nilsen, D.W., Albrektsen, G., Landmark, K., et al. Effects of a high-dose concentrate of n-3 fatty acids or corn oil introduced early after an acute myocardial infarction on serum triacylglycerol and HDL cholesterol. American Journal of Clinical Nutrition 2001; 74: 50-6.

Niu, S.L., Mitchell, D.C., Lim, S.Y., et al. Reduced G protein-coupled signaling efficiency in retinal rod outer segments in response to n-3 fatty acid deficiency. Journal of Biological Chemistry 2004; 279: 31098-104.

Norrish, A.E., Jackson, R.T., Sharpe, S.J., Skeaff, C.M. Men who consume vegetable oils rich in monounsaturated fat: their dietary patterns and risk of prostate cancer. Cancer Causes and Control 2000; 11: 609-15.

Norrish, A.E., Skeaff, C.M., Arribas, G.L., et al. Prostate cancer risk and consumption of fish oils: a dietary biomarker-based case-control study. British Journal of Cancer 1999; 81: 1238-42.

Nyby, M.D., Hori, M.T., Ormsby, B., et al. Eicosapentaenoic acid inhibits Ca2+ mobilization and PKC activity in vascular smooth muscle cells. American Journal of Hypertension 2003; 16: 708-14.

Oddy, W.H. Ratio of omega-6 to omega-3 fatty acids and childhood asthma. Journal of Asthma 2004; 41(3): 319-26.

Oh, K., Hu, F.B., Manson, J.E., et al. Dietary fat intake and risk of coronary heart disease in women: 20 years of follow-up of the nurse's health study. American Journal of Epidemiology 2005; 161: 672-79.

Okie, S. New York to Trans fats: you're out! New England Journal of Medicine 2007; 356: 2017-21.

Olsen, S.F. Is supplementation with marine omega-3 fatty acids during pregnancy a useful tool in the prevention of preterm birth? Clinical Obstetrics and gynecology 2004; 47: 768-74.

Oomen, C.M., Ocke, M.C., Feskens, E.J., et al. Association between trans fatty acid intake and 10-year risk of coronary heart disease in the Zutphen elderly study: a prospective population-based study. Lancet 2001; 357: 746-51.

O'Shea, M., Lawless, F., Stanton, C., Devery, R. Conjugated linoleic acid in bovine milk fat: a food-based approach to cancer prevention. Food Science Technology 1998; 9: 192-6.

Pacht, E.R., DeMichele, S.J., Nelson, J.L., et al. Enteral nutrition with eicosapentaenoic acid, gamma-linolenic acid, and antioxidants reduces alveolar inflammatory mediators and protein influx in patients with acute respiratory distress syndrome. Critical Care Medicine 2003; 31: 491-500.

Pariza, M.W., Park, Y., Cook, M.E. The biologically active isomers of conjugated linoleic acid. Progress in Lipid Research 2001; 40: 283-298.

Parodi, P.W. Conjugated linoleic acid. Food Australia 2002; 54: 96-99.

Phillipson, B.E., Rothrock, D.W., Connor, W.E., et al. Reduction of plasma lipids, lipoproteins, and apoproteins by dietary fish oils in patients with hypertryglceridemia. New England Journal of Medicine 1985; 312: 1210-6.

Pietinen, P., Ascherio, A., Korhonen, P., et al. Intake of fatty acids and risk of coronary heart disease in a cohort of Finnish men. The alpha-tocopherol, beta-carotene cancer prevention study. American Journal of Epidemiology 1997; 145: 876-87.

Pischon, T., Hankinson, S.E., Buring, J.E., et al. Habitual dietary intake of n-3 and n-6 fatty acids in relation to inflammatory markers among US men and women. Circulation 2003; 108: 155-60.

Prescott, S.L. N-3 polyunsaturated fatty acids and allergic disease. Current Opinion in Clinical Nutrition and Metabolic Care 2004; 7(2): 123-9.

Psota, T.L., Gebauer, S.K., Kris-Etherton, P. Dietary omega-3 fatty acid intake and cardiovascular risk. American Journal of Cardiology 2006; 98: 3i-18i.

Raaitt, M.H., Connor, W.E., Morris, C., et al. Fish oil supplementation and risk of ventricular tachycardia and ventricular fibrillation in patients with implantable defibrillators: a randomized controlled trial. Journal of the American Medical Association 2005; 293: 2884-91.

Rainer, L., Heiss, C.J. Conjugated linoleic acid: health implications and effects on body composition. Journal of the American Dietetic Association 2004; 104: 963-8.

Ramos, E.J., Middleton, F.A., Laviano, A., et al. Effects of omega-3 fatty acid supplementation on tumor-bearing rats. Journal of the American College of Surgeons. 2004; 199: 716-23.

Ramos, E.J., Romanova, I.V., Suzuki, S., et al. Effects of omega-3 fatty acids on orexigenic and anorexigenic modulators at the onset of anorexia. Brain Research 2005; 1046: 157-64.

Ravnskov, Uffe. The Cholesterol Myths: Exposing the fallacy that saturated fat and cholesterol cause heart disease. New Trends Publishing, 2000.

Raygada, M., Cho, E., Hilakivi-Clarke, L. High maternal intake of polyunsaturated fatty acids during pregnancy in mice alters offsprings' aggressive behavior, immobility in the swim test, locomotor activity and brain protein kinase C activity. Journal of Nutrition 1998; 128: 2505-11.

Reece, M.S., McGregor, J.A., Allen, K.G., Harris, M.A. Maternal and perinatal long-chain fatty acids: possible roles in preterm birth. American Journal of Obstetrics and Gynecology 1997; 176: 907-14.

Reinwald, S., Li, Y., Moriguchi, T., et al. Repletion with n-3 fatty acids reverses bone deficits in n-3-depleted rats. Journal of Nutrition 2004; 134: 388-94.

Robinson, D.R. Urakaze, M., Huang, R., et al. Dietary marine lipids suppress continuous expression of interleukin-1 beta gene transcription. Lipids 1996; 31(Suppl): s23-s31.

Robinson, J.G., Stone, N.J. Antiatherosclerotic and anti-thrombotic effects of omega-3 fatty acids. The American Journal of Cardiology 2006; 98: 39i-49i.

Rodriguez, B.L., Sharp, D.S., Abbott, R.D., et al. Fish intake may limit the increase in risk of coronary heart disease morbidity and mortality among heavy smokers. The Honolulu Heart Program. Circulation 1996; 94: 952-6.

Rodriguez-Cruz, M., Tovar, A.R., del Prado, M., Torres, N. Molecular mechanisms of action and health benefits of polyunsaturated fatty acids. Revista de Investigacion Clinica 2005; 57: 457-72.

Romano, C., Cucchiara, S., Barabino, A., et al. Usefulness of omega-3 fatty acid supplementation in addition to mesalizine in maintaining remission in pediatric Crohn's disease: a double-blind, randomized, placebo-controlled study. World Journal of Gastroenterology 2005; 11: 7118-21.

Rose, D.P., Connolly, J.M. Effects of fatty acids and eicosanoid synthesis inhibitors on the growth of two human prostate cancer cell lines. Prostate 1991; 18: 243-54.

Ross, J.A., Maingay, J.P., Fearon, K.C., et al. Eicosapentaenoic acid perturbs signaling via the NF kappa-B transcriptional pathway in pancreatic tumour cells. International Journal of Oncology 2003; 23: 1733-8.

Roynette, C.E., Calder, P.C., Dupertuis, Y.M., Pichard, C. n-3 polyunsaturated fatty acids and colon cancer prevention. Clinical Nutrition 2004; 23: 139-51.

Sacks, F.M., Stone, P.H., Gibson, C.M., et al. The HARP research group. Controlled trial of fish oil for regression of human coronary atherosclerosis. Journal of the American College of Cardiology 1995; 25: 1492-8.

Salam, M.T., Li, Y.F., Langholz, B., Gilliland, F.D. Maternal fish consumption during pregnancy and risk of early childhood asthma. The Journal of Asthma 2005; 42: 513-8.

Saugstad, L.F. Are neurodegenerative disorder and psychotic manifestations avoidable brain dysfunctions with adequate dietary omega-3? Nutrition and Health 2006; 18: 89-101.

Saur, L.A., Dauchy, R.T., Blask, D.E. Mechanism for the antitumor and anticachectic effects of n-3 fatty acids. Cancer Research 2000; 60: 5289-95.

Schmid, Ron. The untold story of milk: Green pastures, contented cows, and raw dairy foods. New Trends Publishing, 2003.

Schmocker, C., Weylandt, K.H., Kahlke, L., et al. Omega-3 fatty acids alleviate chemically induced acute hepatitis by suppression of cytokines. Hepatology 2007; 45: 864-9.

Shoelson, S. E., Lee, J., Goldfine, A.B. Inflammation and insulin resistance. Journal of Clinical Investigation 2006; 116: 1793-1801.

Simopoulos, A.P. Essential fatty acids in health and chronic disease. American Journal of Clinical Nutrition 1999; 70: 560s-9s.

Simopoulos, A.P. Omega-3 fatty acids in inflammation and autoimmune diseases. Journal of American College of Nutrition 2002; 21(6): 495-505.

Singh, M. Essential fatty acids, DHA and human brain. Indian Journal of Pediatrics 2005; 72: 239-42.

Singh, R.B., Dubnov, G., Niaz, M.A., et al. Effect of an Indo-Mediterranean diet on progression of coronary artery disease in high risk patients (Indo-Mediterranean Diet Heart Study) A randomized single-blind trial. Lancet 2002; 360: 1455-61.

Singh, R.B., Niaz, M.A., Sharma, J.P., et al. Randomized, double-blind, placebo-controlled trial of fish oil and mustard oil in patients with suspected acute myocardial infarction: the Indian experiment of infarct survival. Cardiovascular Drugs and Therapeutics 1997; 11: 485-91.

Siscovick, D.S., Raghunathan, T.E., King, I. et al. dietary intake and cell membrane levels of long-chain n-3 poly-unsaturated fatty acids and the risk of primary cardiac arrest. Journal of the American Medical Association 1995; 274: 1363-7.

Soyland, E., Funk, J., Rajka, G., et al. Dietary supplementa-tion with very long chain n-3 fatty acids in patients with atopic dermatitis: a double-blind, multi-centre study. British Journal of Dermatology 1994; 130: 757-64.

Soyland, E., Lea, T., Sandstad, B., Drevon, A. Dietary supplementation with very long chain n-3 fatty acids in man decreases expression of the interleukin-2 receptor (CD25) on mitogen-stimulated lymphocytes from patients with inflammatory skin disease. Journal of Clinical Investigation 1994; 24: 236-42.

Spector, S.L., Surette, M.E. Diet and asthma: Has the role of dietary lipids been overlooked in the management of asthma? Annals of Allergy and Immunology 2003; 90: 371-77.

Sperling, R.I., Benincaso, A.I., Knoell, C.T., et al. Dietary omega-3 polyunsaturated fatty acids inhibit phosphoinositide formation and chemotaxis in neutrophils. Journal of Clinical Investigation 1993; 91: 651-60.

Stender, S., Dyerber, J. Influence of trans fatty acids on health. Nutrition and Metabolism 2004; 48: 61-6.

Stenson, W.F., Cort, D., Rodgers, J., et al. Dietary supplementation with fish oil in ulcerative colitis. Annals of Internal Medicine 1992; 116: 609-14.

Stevens, L.J., Zentall, S.S., Deck, J.L., et al. Essential fatty acid metabolism in boys with attention-deficit hyperactivity disorder. American Journal of Clinical Nutrition. 1995; 62: 761-8.

Sundrarjun, T., Komindr, S., Archararit, N., et al. Effects of n-3 fatty acids on serum interleukin-6, tumor necrosis factor-alpha and soluble tumour necrosis factor receptor p55 in active rheumatoid arthritis. Journal of International Medical Research 2004; 32: 443-54.

Sundram, K., Ismail, A., Hayes, K.C., et al. Trans (elaidic) fatty acids adversely affect the lipoprotein profile relative to specific saturated fatty acids in humans. Journal of Nutrition 1997; 127: 514s-20s.

Svegliati-Baroni, G., Candelaresi, C., Saccomanno, S., et al. A model of insulin resistance and nonalcoholic steatohepatitis in rats: role of peroxisome proliferator-activated receptor-alpha and n-3 polyunsaturated fatty acid treatment on liver injury. American Journal of Pathology 2006; 169: 846-60.

Switzer, K.C., McMurray, D.N., Chapkin, R.S. Effects of dietary n-3 polyunsaturated fatty acids on T-cell membrane composition and function. Lipids 2004; 39: 1163-70.

Temme, E.H., Mensink, R.P., Hornstra, G. Comparison of the effects of diets enriched in lauric, palmitic, or oleic acids on serum lipids and lipoproteins in healthy women and men. American Journal of Clinical Nutrition 1996; 63: 897-903.

Terry, P., Lichtenstein, P., Teychting, M., et al. Fatty fish consumption and risk of prostate cancer. Lancet 2001; 357: 1764-6.

Terry, P.D., Terry, J.B., Rohan, T.E. Long-chain (n-3) fatty acid intake and risk of cancers of the breast and the prostate: recent epidemiological studies, biological mechanisms, and directions for future research. Journal of Nutrition 2004; 134: 3412s-20s.

Thies, F., Miles, E.A., Nebe-von-Caron, G., et al. Influence of dietary supplementation with long-chain n-3 or n-6 polyunsaturated fatty acids on blood inflammatory cell populations and functions and on plasma soluble adhesion molecules in healthy adults. Lipids 2001; 36: 1183-93.

Trebble, T.M., Wooton, S.A., Miles, E.A., et al. Prostaglandin E2 production and T cell function after fish-oil supplementation: Response to antioxidant cosupplementation. American Journal of Clinical Nutrition 2003; 78: 376-82.

Tsai, C.J., Leitzmann, M.F., Willett, W.C., Giovannucci, E.L. The effect of long-term intake of cis unsaturated fats on the risk for gallstone disease in men: a prospective cohort study. Annals of Internal Medicine 2004; 141: 514-22.

Tsujikawa, T. Clinical importance of n-3 fatty acid-rich diet and nutritional education for the maintenance of remission in Crohn's disease. Journal of Gastroenterology 2000; 35(2): 99-104.

Valenzuela, A., Morgado, N. Trans fatty acid isomers in human health and in the food industry. Biology Research 1999; 32: 273-87.

Vicario, M., Pedragosa, E., Rivero, M., et al. Dietary unsaturated long-chain fatty acids modify D-glucose absorption in weaning rats. Journal of Pediatric Gastroenterology and Nutrition 2005; 40: 151-6.

Von Schacky, C., Angerer, P., Kothny, W., et al. The effect of dietary omega-3 fatty acids on coronary atherosclerosis: a randomized, double-blind, placebo-controlled trial. Annals of Internal Medicine 1999; 130: 554-62.

Wang, Y., Storlien, L.H., Jenkins, A.B., et al. Dietary variables and glucose tolerance in pregnancy. Diabetes Care 2000; 23: 460-4.

Weber, P.C. Clinical studies on the effects of n-3 fatty acids on cells and eicosanoids in the cardiovascular system. Journal of Internal Medicine Supplement 1989; 225: 61-8.

Weber, P.C., Leaf, A. Cardiovascular effects of omega-3 fatty acids. Atherosclerosis risk factor modification by omega-3 fatty acids. World Review of Nutrition and Dietetics 1991; 66: 218-32.

Wirfalt, E., Mattisson, I., Gullberg, B., et al. Fat from different foods show diverging relations with breast cancer risk in postmenopausal women. Nutrition and Cancer 2005; 53: 135-43.

Wong, K.W. Clinical efficacy of n-3 fatty acid supplementation in patient with asthma. Journal of the American Dietetic Association 2005; 105(1): 98-105.

www.americanheart.org/print_presenter.html Fish and Omega-3 Fatty Acids: American Heart Association Recommendations. Extracted April 25, 2007.

www.benbest.com/lifest/causes.html Causes of Death by Ben Best. Extracted April 19, 2007.

www.bpso.org/practice.htm Practice parameters for the assessment and treatment of children and adolescents with bipolar disorder. Extracted June 7, 2007.

www.cdc.gov//ncipc/factsheets/suifacts.htm Suicide: fact sheet. Extracted June 10, 2007.

www.cfsan.fda.gov/~dms/qatransqatrans2.html   Public
health: chewing the fat on trans fat. Extracted June 19,
2007.

www.cfsan.fda.gov/~frf/sean-mehg.html Mercury levels in
commercial fish and shellfish. Extracted June 19, 2007.

www.fao.org/docrep/T4660T/T4660T02.HTM   Experts'
recommendations on fats and oils in human nutrition.
Extracted June 19, 2007.

ww.nimh.nih.gov/publicat/numbers.cfm?textSize=M   The
numbers count: mental disorders in America. Extracted
June 10, 2007.

www.seer.cancer.gov/statfacts/html/all_print.html   Cancer
stat fact sheets – cancer of all sites: extracted May 1,
2007.

www.unu.edu/unupress/food/8f174e/174e04.htm
Constituents of human milk: extracted June 24, 2007.

www.wikipedia.org/wili/Saturated_fat   Saturated   fat:
extracted June 26, 2007.

Zaloga, G.P., Marik, P. Lipid modulation and systemic
inflammation Critical Care Clinics 2001; 17: 201-17.

Zhao, Y., Joshi-Barve, S., Barve, S., Chen, L.H.
Eicosopentaenoic acid prevents LPS-induced TNF-alpha
expression by preventing NF-kappaB activation. Journal
of American College of Nutrition 2004; 23: 71-78.

Printed in the United States
94263LV00001B/154-1500/A